MW01280131

While Other
Children Played

I Have Lived

In early childhood life depended
    on silence, I lived
I have lived Anne Frank's
    fears and terrors
I have lived Solzhenitsyn's
    crippling cold, hunger, and pain
I have lived Eli Wiesel's loss of
    a parent, just as freedom lie ahead
I have lived guilt, hatred, and
    extreme shame
I lived
I have lived Victor Hugo's
    Les Miserables
I lived

I have lived love and having
    wonderful children
I have lived the pain of cancer
    when it strikes loved ones
I have lived financial comfort
    and easy living
The beauty of sunsets and
    quieting waters

I have lived
I have lived true agony and
    hopelessness of depression
I lived
Destiny has dealt me a generous hand
    in this fabulous life
Oh, how I have lived

            —Erna Gorman

While Other Children Played

A Hidden
Child
Remembers
the Holocaust

ERNA GORMAN

Edited by Barbara J. Krügel
Foreword by Dr. Sidney M. Bolkosky

Voice/Vision Holocaust Survivor Oral History Archive
University of Michigan-Dearborn

University of Michigan-Dearborn
4901 Evergreen Rd.
Dearborn, MI 48128

Managing Editor: Terri Schell
Art Director: Mary Claire Krzewinski

ISBN 10: 0-933691-15-7
ISBN 13: 978-0-933691-15-5

Library of Congress Control Number: 2010929230

Printed in the United States of America
All rights reserved
10 9 8 7 6 5 4 3 2 1

I dedicate this book to

my husband, Herb,

my three children, Mark, Robert, and his wife Ruth,

my grandchildren, Julia, Lily, and Sydney.

I am grateful for their unwavering support and love.

CONTENTS

CONTENTS

Epilogue [187]

Survivors have difficulty relating their experiences for a variety of reasons, from the obvious emotional stress of recounting such memories, to the failure of language to communicate that horrible reality. Forced to use words that do not resonate with their listeners—words overflowing with meanings—and unable to convey the simultaneity of events that involve a conglomeration of smells, sights, feelings, sounds, and other physical and emotional phenomena, many survivors have opted not to speak. How is it possible to describe the details of the minute-to-minute, hour-to-hour tedium and utter fear? Can listeners appreciate the smells that Erna depicts—the refuse bucket, the water, the animals? Can anyone fathom the impact that hearing the sounds of other children playing had on a dejected young girl? Feel the hay as she recalls its odor and its touch? Grasp the silence? "We could not talk. ... Even at night you shouldn't talk because what if somebody crawls against the wall of the barn and hears you? We became animals.... It cannot be reality."

We may not ever fathom the complete stories of survivors. But we will rarely come closer than we do when listening to Erna. She exudes her humanity, draws us in, invites our sympathy. Her tone shines through in this narrative, in part because Barbara Kriigel's editorial support captured it with a compassion that met Erna's. Haunted as Erna may be by her memories, she has learned to cope with the trauma she experienced, and this is perhaps the final piece of her long education. Her resilience should astonish us, as she overcomes the difficulty of living in two worlds simultaneously.

Sidney M. Bolkosky
William E. Stirton Professor in the Social Sciences
University of Michigan-Dearborn
January 2010

INTRODUCTION

I t took me more than 35 years to begin talking about my experiences as a hidden child during the Holocaust. People sometimes wonder why I waited so long to tell the story of how I survived. Even my husband and two sons did not know the details of what I had endured; they only knew that my family and I were forced into hiding and that I was a survivor. In hindsight, I can point to two events, several years apart, that made me realize I could no longer suppress the story of the many horrific things that happened to my family, changing our lives forever.

The first event that caused me to reflect on my life was my father's death in 1977. He had been a major presence in my life, and suddenly he was no longer with me. Questions I should have asked him or conversations we should have had were no longer possible. There are many gaps in my recollections and the documentation I have. My efforts to organize my family's history would have been so much easier if I could talk with him and ask if my memories and feelings are accurate, why or when certain events occurred, and how he managed to save us.

The second event occurred several years later, when I saw a television interview of an American "skinhead." He was a young, athletic, good-looking boy, dressed in a

German military uniform. He stood with a raised arm and declared, "I'm here to finish Hitler's work." Another interview featured a young man spouting white supremacist slogans while standing next to a mother holding a child on her lap. However, it was the first skinhead's statement, "I'm here to finish Hitler's work," that stuck in my mind and petrified me. It was as if he were saying that I, Erna Gorman, had no right to live. Although he didn't specifically say he hated Jews, his statement suggested to me that he believed my family and I had no right to exist because we were Jewish. I couldn't get over it! My wonderful sons who were already in college had no right to exist? How could this be? Yet here was this young man spewing hatred against people he didn't even know.

My immediate physical response was to lose control of my bladder, a problem I had frequently experienced during and immediately after the war whenever I felt afraid or threatened. This problem hadn't occurred in over thirty years, but the skinhead's statement revived all my childhood fears and resulted in an intense physical and emotional reaction.

These events sent me into a tailspin. I began to recall and dwell upon all the horrible things that had happened to me; little by little, I became very sad and depressed. Although part of my mind knew I was now safe from harm, the other part said something totally opposite. Eventually I had to seek professional help so I could reconcile my memories of many unthinkable childhood experiences.

Since that time, I have told my story to thousands of people, to adults and children, to individuals and groups. I don't tell my story to gain sympathy or pity but to help explain the effects of hatred and discrimination on a single individual. When I tell my story, I do not read from a script; my story is told differently each time, and I put a lot of feeling and emotion into what I share. Sometimes I speak more coherently than other times, and sometimes I connect better to the audience; each telling is unique. I particularly like talking to young people. I feel that if I can help them understand the pain and suffering of others, then I can help them stand up for those who are being bullied, make them recognize that we are all human, and help them learn to act more kindly toward each other. Today we constantly hear stories of children who have been tormented by their peers in school. Sometimes the bullied victims resort to violence against their classmates; sometimes they resort to killing themselves. The message I try to convey to young people about tolerance and understanding each other's pain is a message they need to hear and embrace. This lesson needs to be taught over and over again, and they need to hear it from everyone around them.

Some might think that telling my story is a catharsis for me, but it isn't. It is destructive to keep thinking about these events and re-experiencing the emotions that come with the memories. I'm not a teacher; I'm not a psychologist or a preacher. I can only tell others how I feel and how I lived my life as a result of what happened to me. That is the only thing I can do. My husband and sons hope that by writing this down, I can stop telling my stories so that I don't become so upset. Perhaps this will enable me to retire from speaking to groups. Perhaps I can finally stop reliving the Holocaust. Perhaps not.

In my memories, I don't see myself as a child at all. The only *mental* picture I have of myself is as a grown-up person with grown-up pains and grown-up feelings. Sometimes my memories are in the third person, almost as if I am two different people. I really don't feel like this happened to me, Erna; I'm so far removed. If I cry, I cry for this other person, not for me. I cry for the person who experienced this, but this person is separated from me. Is this logical? I don't know; it doesn't make any sense except to me. Maybe separating myself from this other person is a method of coping and survival even today.

The story I am going to tell includes memories I distinctly recall. Some parts of the story were told to me by others. My memories mostly involve my parents and myself; I'm not sure why I don't remember more about my sister, Suzanne. It's funny, but she once told me that she doesn't really have many memories of me from this time either. Perhaps it's because there was a six-year difference in our ages; perhaps it's because we were each so traumatized by the events. She never wanted to discuss what happened and only agreed to share her memories with me on three occasions, many years after the fact. I have a number of pieces of documentation; some were re-created after the war in order for my father, my sister, and me to re-establish our identities. Photos were accumulated through various relatives who had survived or were not in the Holocaust.

I very much regret that I didn't write these things down sooner when I could easily recall places or names. This regret has also inspired action. I have to do it now, before it is too late.

Every story needs to be put into its appropriate context, with the joys and fears that existed at the time. Painful stories like mine aren't told because of ego or to build self-esteem but because of a genuine hope that readers can learn a lesson. Even small stories are written to teach something, to share feelings or provide insight into history, or perhaps to simply organize and detail a series of events.

Sometimes I have only impressions or feelings about what transpired. Children do not always remember things accurately. The feelings about events and relationships are very complex, and while my recollections may not always be accurate, they are what I'm left with at the end of the day. I will do my best to tell what I know and what I feel about the *miracle* of my family's survival.

Blitzer

1°

Nom :

Suzanne

1928 Décéd

à

N

évrier 1929

Service,

Rodhain

Prénoms :

16 Août

My Family

I was born in Metz, France, on August 16, 1934, to Malka and Leib Blitzer. My sister, Suzanne, was about six years old at the time. My mother came from Monasterzyska in the Ukraine, a region that was at times a part of Poland, and at other times a part of the Soviet Union; my father was from Rozwadów in southeastern Poland. Both of my parents left their home villages to live and work in France. My mother lived with her sister Cella, but I'm not sure where my father lived. I have no idea how my parents met, but I believe my father knew of my mother's family back in the Ukraine. Perhaps they were like other immigrants, eager to know other people from their home country.

Left: Suzanne, age 9, and me, age 3, in France, around 1937. Center: Birth records for Suzanne and me. Right: My parents, Malka and Leib Blitzer, in the mid-1920s.

My father was a less-than-successful merchant, selling clothes. Documentation I have shows my parents' marriage was officially recorded in France in 1929, but I believe they were actually married in a religious ceremony several years earlier.

My mother, Malka, was born on October 4, 1902, to Shoshana (nee Blech) and Salomon Antler. She was the second of ten children, six girls and four boys. The family lived in a very small house and was not prosperous; I've heard that my grandfather sold goods from a pushcart. My mother and three of her siblings, Cella, Regina, and Ojser, had each moved to France before World War II. None of my mother's family who remained in Poland survived the war; I don't know for sure how they died. In France, my aunts Cella and Regina managed to survive the war, but my Uncle Ojser, who lived in Paris, was taken to Drancy, a concentration camp in northern France, when the Nazis began gathering the Jews for deportation. Documentation lists him as a member of Convoy 6, which left from Pithiviers, France, on July 17, 1942. Convoy 6 arrived in Auschwitz on July 19, 1942. Both the men and women of the convoy were assigned numbers (men's numbers ranged from 48,880 to 49,688), so it is evident that they weren't immediately murdered, but by 1945 there were only 45 survivors from this convoy, and my uncle was not among them.

My father was born Leib Krolik on May 27, 1897, to Esther (nee Blitzer) and Joseph Krolik, in the small town of Pyschnyca. Known as Jacob, he was one of the youngest of eight children, three boys and five girls. When he was very young, the family moved to Rozwadów, where they prospered; they lived in a large home in a corner of the town square. The main house had a courtyard surrounded by smaller apartments that were occupied by various family members, and there were a number of stores in front of the building. Suzanne told me that she remembered the large house having very long corridors that led to many rooms, but she didn't really remember much else about the building. (After the war, my French cousin Bernard Kanter, a salesman who had visited Poland numerous times, went back to Rozwadów and found the family complex still standing, although I believe it has since been torn down.) Two of my father's siblings, Louis and Helen, immigrated to the United States before the war began. My father's handwriting was beautiful, an indication that he did have a good education. At some point, my father had a terrible argument with my grandfather that ended with my grandfather slapping him. This prompted my father to leave home and change his surname from Krolik to his mother's maiden name, Blitzer. So Leib Krolik became Leib Blitzer, known later as Leon Blitzer and finally as Jack Blitzer. It can be quite complicated when I talk about my father's family because some of his siblings used the original name Krolik and others used the name Blitzer. The documentation trail can also be difficult to follow because of all the name changes. Very confusing!

My paternal grandfather remarried after my grandmother Esther died. My Hebrew name is Esther, so I know she had already died by the time I was born. My grandfather had more children with his second wife, but I don't know their names or dates of birth. I haven't been able to find anything about what happened to my father's family, even though they numbered more than 50. In the early days of the war, the Germans and the local thugs treated the Jews much differently than they did in later years. At the time, Jews weren't put onto transports, and there weren't the large mass killings that occurred later. At first, Jews were taken in small groups to be killed, sometimes a few at a time, sometimes a hundred or more. It is possible that these family members were taken early on to perform forced labor in factories or farms. Maybe they were shot in the forest. I don't know. What amazes me is that there are no records, which leads me to conclude that they were taken by Poles; the Germans kept precise records of such activity, but the Poles did not. In the beginning, the local German commanders were able to treat Jews at their own discretion, helped by the local community. I assume, therefore, that my father's family was killed by the Poles. It wasn't until after the Wannsee Conference in 1942, at which Nazi officials created a coordinated plan to exterminate European Jews, that the mass murder began in earnest.

My grandfather owned a great deal of rental property in Poland. I have a typed, legal-looking list of the various properties he owned before the war; the list was probably recorded with the local government. I also have several letters from some of the tenants who wrote to my father after the war about a dispute regarding bins of coal, so I know there were properties still considered at that time to be held by my father's family. In 1947, my father made a couple of trips to Rozwadów to look for other survivors and also to check on his father's holdings. During those visits he was under constant danger because people who had taken over the various apartments did not want to give up the properties that they had effectively stolen from our family. So even after the war, my father was still afraid for his life. Our family never gained control of the property again, but at this point, I feel no need to pursue recovering those things. People who benefited from the Holocaust don't want others to know, especially in the smaller cities. I never investigated whether or not I could make a claim to what was stolen from us.

Pre-War France

My memories of France before the war are essentially non-existent. The one faint recollection I have involves my mother and the candlesticks she used for Sabbath rituals. Every Jewish family, no matter how poor, had candlesticks. I assume this memory is from the time we lived in France before the war, because during the war all of our possessions were taken. I don't believe my parents were particularly religious, but they did follow Jewish traditions and rituals.

Left: Suzanne and I stand with my mother, around 1937; the purse my mother is holding somehow survived the war, and it is now one of my most cherished possessions.
Background: one of the many arches in my hometown of Metz, France.

My parents were good-looking people, and we were an attractive family. I have pictures of my parents from the time they lived in France as well as photos of them with their parents and siblings. One photo I particularly treasure is of me with my mother and sister, Suzanne. In the photo my mother is holding a purse; amazingly, the purse has survived all these years and is now one of my most cherished possessions. It is all I have left of my mother.

I have pierced ears. My mother probably had this done in Metz while I was a child, maybe as a baby. I remember always wearing my little earrings even when we were hidden during the war. They had some sort of tiny stone in them, and I don't remember ever taking them out except when I was a teenager. At some point after I came to the United States, they became lost; I don't remember losing them, and I can't imagine that I would have thrown them away. I wish I still had them.

Metz had a small Orthodox synagogue that is still standing. A larger German-style synagogue was later built next to it, but the new synagogue is more conservative than Orthodox. Both structures are still side-by-side, but I think the old synagogue was recently turned into a Hebrew school. My Aunt Cella put a plaque in memory of my mother in the old synagogue, and it's still there. The last time I went to the synagogue was in 2006; my granddaughter Julia was with me, and I showed the plaque to her. Whenever I visited these synagogues, I would always go in through the back doors, never the front doors. We

didn't want to be noticed or show ourselves too much, because anti-Semitism has always been a problem in France;
even now, after all these years, we always stay low-key to
avoid notice.

Mogielnica
Wyśmierzyce
Żelechów
Kock
Ra
Wisła
Dęblin
Irena
Baranów
Parczew
Włodawa
Prypet
Radomka
Radom
Kozienice
Lubartów
Wysokie
Puławy
Ostrów
żywa Nowa
Wy
Skaryszew
Koło
Zwoleń
Kazimierz
Nałęczów
Łęczna
LublinT
Szydłowiec
Iłża
Rybaki
LUBLIN
Opole
L U B L I N
Wierzbnik
Rejowiec
Chełm
Dubienka
zysko-
ienna
Ostrowiec
Kraśnik
Krasnystaw
Bystrzyca
Kielce
Kamienna
Opatów
Wojsławice
Horodło
Hrubieszów
Iwaniska
Zawichost
Janów
Szczebrzeszyn
Zamość
Werl
bkowice
Sandomierz
Rozwadów
Zawada
Tarnobrzeg
Stalowa Wola
Nisko
Tereszpol
Wożuczy
Staszów
Wisko
Tanew
Biłgoraj
Sokal
Busko
Rudnik
Ujanów
Tomaszów Lub.
Uhnów
Bełz
Mielec
POLAND
Wielkie
Radomyśl Wk.
Sokołów
Leżajsk
Sieniawa
Rawa Ruska
Rata
Dąbrowa
Kolbuszowa
Głogów
Lubaczów
Niemirów
Kulików
Żabno
Dębica
Lancut
Przeworsk
Żółkiew
Tarnów
Rzeszów
Jarosław
Jaworów
Jaryczów
Ropczyce
Kańczuga
Radymno
Krakowiec
Janów
LWÓ
Pilzno
Tyczyn
Strzyżów
Błażowa
Dynów
Mościska
Gródek
Winniki
Jasło
Brzostek
L
W
O
Przemyśl
Sądowa Wisznia
Szczerzec
Gorlice
Brzozów
Niżankowice
Rudkio
Komarno
Mikołaja
Grybów
Rymanów
Dobromil
Sambor
Krosno
Sanok
Chyrów
Strwiąż
Dukla
Lesko
Stara Sól
Drohobycz
Nowy Sącz(Alt Sandec)
Ustrzyki Dolne
Stary Sambor
Borysław
nica-Zdrój
Muszyna
Łupków
Cisna
Truskawiec
Turka
Skole
Kałusz
Humenne
Sianki
Uźok
Tuchla
Satoraljaújhely
Čop
Mukačevo
Latorica
Berehovo
Chust
Kralovo

I used to pull on his *payes* (sidecurls); this was a great pleasure, and I still enjoy thinking about it. Sometimes my grandfather held my hand and walked with me to the synagogue for services. Children were allowed to remain with the men during services, but since I was small, all I could see were coats and legs in black pants. It was a tiny room. I remember the men with huge *tallitot* (prayer shawls) draped over their heads as they chanted and *shuckled* (rocked back and forth). The women also prayed, separated from the men by a curtain. These are good memories.

On Fridays, my father had us put our heads together, and then he placed his hands above our heads and said a blessing. Once he even held a chicken over our heads to ward off the evil; however, the chicken gave me a scare and a chill! I now think that this was a sign of how desperate my father must have felt, because for a modern man to resort to a superstitious act like that indicates that he was willing to try anything to protect us.

I don't recall having any friends or playing with other children while we were with my maternal grandparents. I never had a doll. When I later spoke about my memories with my sister, she also could not remember playing. My only memories of playing or being cuddled are when I was with my grandfather. I was a serious child and not boisterous.

Tensions grew very quickly in this little house, which was now part of the ghetto. Voices were hushed, and I was often told to stay quiet. I was constantly warned not to go out and ordered to hide if someone came into the house. Curtains were drawn over the small windows, even during the day. My aunts knew how to sew, and the *Judenrat* (a committee of Jewish men who governed the local Jewish population, under Nazi orders) gave them a daily quota of shirts to make for German soldiers, an indication that our area was indeed now a ghetto. My aunts and uncles were always coming and leaving, coming and leaving, as was my father. Despite this constant activity, there was a hush over everything. I likely was not aware of what was happening politically at that time, and if I was, I have blocked it out. But it was obvious that something bad was about to happen that had to do with the fact that we were Jewish.

The cramped conditions soon made it impossible for the extended family to live together, and my parents found us a little apartment—a room, really—that was part of a larger house. A German officer lived in the main house, and we were in the back. We were always quiet; I don't think the captain even knew we were there. During the time when we were still permitted to walk outside, I remember being out with my mother and seeing German soldiers with long coats tipping their hats to her because she was very beautiful. This must have been before the *Aktionen* (the systematic capture and deportation of Jews to concentration camps) began taking place. After a while, I wasn't allowed outside anymore. It was too dangerous. Despite the fact that restrictions on Jews were becoming increasingly severe, my father tried to find odd jobs to help pay for expenses, and at one point I think he worked in a lumberyard.

Rumors that something dire was about to happen were constant, and my father must have determined that he needed to make plans for our safety. The Germans conducted several *Aktionen* in Monasterzyska, searching house-to-house for Jews to arrest. Jews deemed able to work were sent to forced-labor or concentration camps. The very young and old were disposed of in other ways, never to be seen again. Groups of Jews were frequently taken to a forest where they were forced to dig a common grave, and then they were shot. I can only assume that when the German militia came to the front of our house, they saw the name of the German captain and decided to bypass us.

Eventually my grandparents and most of the other family members were taken away, and we never saw them again. Some family members were supposedly sent to Bergen-Belsen, but we were not sure who. On one occasion, my father was taken away, and my panicked family thought he had been shot. He soon returned with his head shaved, and he told us that he had been forced to bury people in a mass grave; among the dead were my mother's family. As he embraced us, he and my mother recited the prayer for the dead, the *Kaddish*. Both of them were crying. I'm not sure exactly where we were when this occurred; many details around this time of confusion are unclear to me.

ołów
zowa Leżajsk   Sieniawa   Cieszanów   Most   ty Wielkie
Głogów   Lubaczów   Rawa Ru: ska   Rato
Lanut   Przeworsk   Niemirów   Żółkiew   Kulików
Rzeszów   Jarosław   Jaworów   Jaryczów
Kańczuga   Radymn   Krakowiec   Szkło   Jaworów   Jaryczów
ów   L   W   O   Janów   W   Lwo
ynów   Mościska   Gród el   Winniki
Brzozów   Przemyśl   Sądowa   Jagi   Szczerzec
Niżankowice   Wisznia   Rudkio
anów   Dobromil   Strwiąż   Komarndo   Mikołajów
Sanok   Chyrów   Sambor   Dniess   Rozdó
Lesko   Stara Sól   Drohobycz   ydaczów
Ustrzyki Dolne   Stan   Stary
Sambor   Borysław   SStryj   Świca
Łupków   Truskawiec   Stryj   Bolechów
Cisna   Turka   S   Kałusz
umenne   Skole   Dolina   St
umpelctz)   Sianki   S   T   A   N   (S
Uzok   Tuchla
Michalovce   Ławoczne   UKR
Użhorod   Vrecky Pass   Volovec   Por Jutyg   Lomnica
K   Svaljava   Popadja 5,715
Latorica   U   Rafa
Cop   Mukačevo   I   N
Tisza   A   T   Jablonicky Pa
Berehovo   A   Jasina (Körösme
Szamos   Kralovo   Chust   Rahovo
reg háza   Satu   Sighet
POLAND

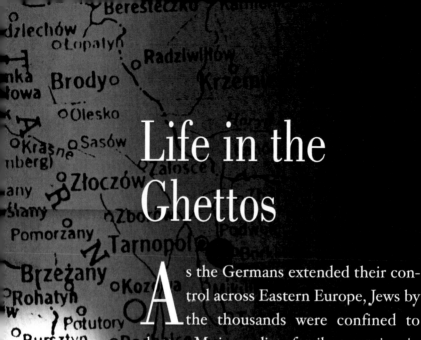

Life in the Ghettos

As the Germans extended their control across Eastern Europe, Jews by the thousands were confined to ghettos. My immediate family spent time in several ghettos. I don't know the names of all of them, how long we were there, or the order of the ghettos. I do know that conditions in the ones that I do recall, including Monasterzyska, Buczacz, and Borky, were especially harsh. Near the end of our ordeal, we were also in Skallat. I don't have any recollections about how we were transported between ghettos, but I believe the distances were not great.

My family escaped the danger of Rozwadów and eventually landed in Monasterzyska (highlighted), a city just east of Poland's border with the Ukraine, where my mother's family lived. (Map by Hammond World Atlas.)

My memories of the ghettos involve quiet, stillness, fear, and hunger. As young as I was, I knew that it was better not to be seen. I knew that I had to run to wherever I was going in order to lessen the chance of being seen. To survive in the ghetto, it was important to remain insignificant. I remember people disappearing, never to be heard from again. I once saw a body with a gash to the neck so severe that I thought the head had been cut off. This horrifying experience had such an impact on me that I remember it to this day, even though I don't recall the adults reacting with the same horror that I did. Each time we escaped one of the many *Aktionen*, we knew it was just a fluke; there was no logic or pattern to detect. However, rumors that an *Aktion* was about to happen were constant. Somehow someone would receive a warning—perhaps it was from the *Judenrat*, I don't know. We knew we needed a place to hide in order to survive, but we couldn't use the same place more than once or twice because the Germans became more adept at discovering where people might be hidden; we were always planning ahead. As circumstances grew worse, there were no more warnings. Since things changed gradually, no one panicked; everyone continued to adapt to the ever-worsening conditions. People watched helplessly as their family members were taken away.

Children, of course, knew even less about what was happening. Adults didn't give explanations to children. I have the sense that my parents either wanted to protect us or they didn't feel the need to explain. It's difficult for me to define "a sense." What does it mean? I have difficulty understanding the word, although I use it a lot. Does it mean that the event was predictable, that someone told me directly, that I overheard it, or that I imagined it? I don't know what it means. But that's the word I use.

One very bad memory I have involves a time when I was playing outside with a young boy. Suddenly, a man and woman ran by us. Soldiers chased after them, and they asked us which direction the couple had gone. We were so petrified that we pointed the way. When I went back into the house, I did not tell anyone about what had happened. The next day, I heard some talk that a couple had been killed, and in my mind, I decided it must have been the people we saw. To this day, I feel very guilty about this incident. Although ultimately I know I'm not responsible for their lives—for them dying—I still have a *sense* of being responsible. The blame that I put on myself is probably of my own creation. Nevertheless, I have been plagued by guilt ever since. I saw other dead people and a few hangings, but nothing stirred the same emotional reaction. Such emotions have no basis in reality; they are totally separated from rational thought. As a result, the burden of responsibility is tremendous. Of course, maybe I am mistaken in my conclusion; maybe it was a coincidence. I never spoke about this with my parents, and I have never been able to come to terms with it.

My recollection is that only one other family member was with us in any of the ghettos, one of my mother's brothers. He was slight and not very tall. The rest of our family had disappeared or been murdered by this point.

For many years, I thought it was possibly my Uncle Aron who was with us. However, several years ago, my French cousin showed me a photo of our Uncle Hertzel, and I instantly recognized him as the man who was with us in the ghetto and helped to save us. My father and uncle used cups to dig a cavity underneath the floorboards of our room in one of the ghettos, perhaps in Buczacz. I have no idea how they managed to get rid of all the dirt without being detected; perhaps they took it out at night. The cavity was large enough for the four of us to sit down, with room for two or three others. I definitely remember knowing that we shouldn't tell anyone about the hiding place we had created. During Nazi attempts to round up Jews, my family hid in this tomb-like place, sometimes for as long as a day or two. My uncle helped us get into the cavity, replaced the floorboards, and then ran away to hide himself. It was very dark, pitch black, with no food and hardly any air to breathe. It was oppressive. I knew I had to be totally quiet because if I wasn't, we would be discovered and everyone would die.

When we hid, my mother brought a pillow. She held my head in her lap and placed the pillow on my back. I now know for certain that my mother would never have harmed me, but at the time, in my child's mind, I became afraid that if I cried out, I would be smothered. I knew that other babies and children had been smothered to keep them quiet, not necessarily by their mothers but by other people in hiding with them, so I was aware that if I were to make any noise, I would put everyone in danger. I remember feeling my mother's body tremble as she held me tightly against her. I had a tremendous fear of the pillow, and it has been present in my nightmares all my life, nightmares from which I would awaken screaming because of the feeling of someone trying to smother me. I never allowed my children to play with pillows, try to smother each other in play, or have a pillow fight. When my grandchildren play with pillows or with couch cushions to make a house or a fort, I always check the structure because I'm afraid the pillows will fall and smother them. To this day, I still can't stand to have a pillow over my head. Unfortunately, I never had the chance to ask my mother about the real purpose of the pillow. Childhood fears are very strong, stronger than logic, and can remain with you for many years. A lifetime.

When it was safe to come out of hiding, someone removed the floorboards, and we emerged once again, usually to find one or two dead bodies nearby. People didn't scream or carry on afterwards; I mostly just remember silence. Perhaps everyone was used to what was happening, or they didn't want to bring attention to themselves, or they already felt defeated; it's hard to know why they remained silent. People get used to shutting out emotions. Silence in a human being does not necessarily indicate a lack of feelings. Sometimes I think that many simply thought, I'm glad it's not me, as selfish as that may seem. Moreover, a public display of emotion was pointless. Most people will do whatever it takes in order to survive; watching people being murdered, therefore, can bring out silence in anyone, if such silence will ensure survival.

43

The second time we used "the tomb," my uncle was shot and killed as he ran away after helping us hide. He saved our lives at the expense of his own; he was a hero. From then on, it was just the four of us trying to survive together.

I recall using the hiding place under the floor a few times. One time, I could hear German militiamen shouting, "*Juden raus!* ("Jews, get out!"). Boots stomped overhead, back and forth, and rifle butts thumped the floor to test for hollowness that might lead to a hiding space. I still remember the sound. Although it may have been my imagination, one time I had the sense that the soldier recognized the hollow sound under his feet and knew there was a cavity but did not give us away. I don't know why I believed this, but it was the sense that I had. I now consider this soldier to be a hero. Not every soldier was a murderer. It makes me believe that there's a chance for humanity because there are people who are kind. I call this *the first miracle of our survival.*

The stench in the tomb was awful because I always lost bladder control. This problem began while we were in the ghettos, before we started hiding in the tomb. I knew our lives were in danger because we were Jewish. Loss of bladder control was a physical manifestation of my fear. I knew I had to behave in a certain way, and I was afraid. Although I could control my cries, my body found other ways to rebel, and I could not control my bladder.

We had a tomb-like hiding place in several of the ghettos. I remember one tomb being just large enough for our family, while others were large enough to accommodate additional people. Another hiding place I recall was a cavity hidden behind an armoire. My parents constantly searched for ways to keep us safe, no matter where we were. That was their primary focus and purpose: to maintain the safety of their children. Maybe that's why I don't remember them talking much to me or hugging me. They were preoccupied with survival.

My sister told me that we all wore white armbands with a blue star; we didn't wear a yellow star on our clothing like people in other places did. Local authorities made the decision regarding what insignia Jews were required to wear, probably based on guidelines given to them. I don't actually remember wearing an armband, but I seem to remember my mother making them.

In one of the ghettos, my father became very ill, probably with typhoid, and I remember him lying in a row with other people who were also very ill. I followed my mother around holding a basin of water as she sponged the various patients. We went around and around, constantly sponging.

Ghetto life was just surviving day-to-day.

Hidden in a Hayloft

Sometime in early 1943, while we were in either Borky or Buczacz, my father somehow made contact with a farmer who agreed to help hide our family. My sister and I later speculated why the farmer was willing to help us, and the only reason we can imagine is that the farmer had heard about America and was interested in going there to live. I am guessing that my father made some sort of promise that if we were to survive the war, he would help the farmer immigrate to the United States with the assistance of my Aunt Helen, who already lived there. Our family had no money, no jewels, and no items of value that the farmer could have wanted. Perhaps he was just a good man, and we were lucky enough to be the ones he helped. It's surely luck, I'm convinced. Everything in my life was just luck.

My husband, Herb, made this painting of my family and the farmer who helped us hide in the hayloft of a barn in the Ukraine.

Whatever the reasons, the farmer agreed to hide our family. I believe this man is in heaven and can hear me as I speak, and he deserves my eternal gratitude. He saved my life. He is proof that one person *can* make a difference in somebody's life. The farmer's willingness to provide us a hiding place is *the second miracle of our survival.*

I don't remember leaving the ghetto, but I do remember running in fields at night in order to get to the farm where we were going to hide. We spent the daylight hours out of sight, tucked into a crevice or ditch somewhere; under cover of night, however, we were on the move.

When we finally arrived at our destination, the farmer and his young wife were waiting for us near the barn. I know the farmer's wife wasn't very happy at all with our presence, and the couple argued about keeping us. Her objections were understandable: we were putting their lives at risk if anyone found out they were hiding Jews in their barn. When I tell people we were hidden in a barn, they usually think of a spacious American-style barn. The barn in which we hid was not like that. It was small, not much more than a shack with a second-level hayloft. Of course, we couldn't see much in the dark barn, but I did notice that the walls of the barn were covered with leaves hung to dry; in fact, I now know that tobacco was a crop grown in the area. There was no livestock in the barn, just some pails and hay and a makeshift ladder on the left-hand side going up to the loft. I remember trying to see what else there was in the barn, but all I could

The seasons in the Ukraine change drastically, and we felt every bit of that change as we lay in the hayloft. Our tiny space was very drafty and cold in the winter, although the hay did provide some insulation. More unbearable were the summers. We were close to the roof line, which baked in the sun, resulting in absolutely stifling heat. During the warm months, I could hear children outside, and at times I thought I could hear splashing. I would close my eyes and transport myself to a place where I was in water or walking in the rain; I would actually feel the rain on me. For years after the war, whenever there was a summer rain, I would go outside and walk, even washing my hair sometimes in the rain. The sensation of the water running down my skin signified freedom.

In summer, the lice became even worse, and the stench was unbearable. Hay becomes different in summer; it has a misty quality I can still smell. However, the hay in the loft wasn't sweet-smelling like the hay below; it was the smell of hell. I recall the hay being changed only once or twice during the two years we were hidden. The smell was horrendous because we were all using a single bucket for elimination, and there was no source of fresh air. The realities of life hidden in the barn—poor hygiene, malnutrition, lack of movement—led to an emptiness, an inability to feel anything. Not fear, not happiness, nothing—no thoughts, just a body without a soul and without a mind, little more than flesh and bones. Still, my body rebelled and refused to be controlled; losing control of my bladder continued to be an issue for me.

One day became another and time slowly passed, and soon even the sense of time was lost beyond the indications of day and night through a crack in the wall. In the late 1970s and early 1980s, when Americans were held hostage in Iran, I sympathized with those captives; I felt everything about my own experience again. They were in isolation and subject to the extremes of heat and cold. I just felt for them so much. This international crisis affected me very personally. In fact, I wrote a letter to Washington, D.C., in support of their release.

By the time our second year of hiding began, I was no longer talking or trying to catch a glimpse of the outside world through the crack; I just lay still and silent on the blanket. The feeling I remember during the second year is total deadness. It's hard to remember much else because the days melded together into nothingness, yet the memory of the lice and vermin remain. Whether there were other important incidents during this time, I don't know; this memory replaces all the other things that might have happened. How my parents coped, I don't know. I'm not sure I could have, as an adult and as a parent. It shows that human beings can endure almost anything. At my age now, I think I would have given up. Most people don't give up, however; human beings have a strong survival instinct. We keep fighting. My sister may have had other memories of this time, but she wasn't willing to talk to me until the last couple years of her life. None of us wanted to deal with our past. Many survivors understandably try to shut these details out of their minds.

Our health was in constant peril. The lice caused terrible infections, and one side of my head was swollen as a result. The wound was terribly painful and took several years after the war to totally heal. At various points, we all had diarrhea; it's even possible that I had typhoid. I became very ill, and I can still picture my mother crying in distress. She begged the farmer to bring some nourishment, some cream or milk, anything to help me. Perhaps she thought I was dying; at least I thought I was dying. My sister frequently developed swollen glands in her neck, and the farmer gave my mother some sort of heated oil that she applied with a cloth. All we could do was lie on the blanket. I don't remember ever lifting the blanket to move the straw around. After a while our muscles began to atrophy, and we became very weak and unable to move.

The farmer regularly fought with his wife about hiding us, and on many occasions my mother resorted to pleading with him to let us stay. The farmer's wife was quite a bit younger than he was, and I assume she was afraid for their children. Indeed, all of their lives were in danger. My parents dealt only with the farmer, never with his wife. More than once, the farmer ordered us to leave. My mother begged on her knees, asking him to let us stay. Another month, just another month, surely the horror would end soon, she argued. In the early days of our ordeal, my mother once disguised herself as a peasant, slipping into town to see if she could find an alternative hiding place. She was unsuccessful, however, and my parents simply told the farmer that they would not go. Perhaps the farmer was deeply religious and thought he wouldn't be able to face God if he forced us to leave. The bravery of this man was incredible.

At one point, the farmer may have become concerned that he was under suspicion of hiding Jews. He opened the barn and let children come in to play in the hay, perhaps as a way of demonstrating his innocence. He put extra bales of hay in front of us, and we crouched in a corner against the roof line. The loft was packed to capacity, and we could barely breathe. We could hear the children playing and jumping in the hay. Afterward, the farmer securely locked the barn again. Another time, either militiamen or Germans came into the barn, poking bayonets into the hay bales that were hiding us. None of us dared to breathe. We could see the hay moving, and one of the bayonets came very close to my head. Fortunately, the soldiers did not take the loft or barn apart, and eventually they left. Few of us believe in miracles, but I am left to wonder, why didn't they burn the barn down? I think this is *another of my miracles of survival*. I ask myself the question, how and why did I survive? I just don't understand it. Maybe we were just meant to survive. People were suspicious, and everyone was watching each other, especially in that area. When people "in the know" learn that I was hidden near Buczacz, in the Tarnopol area, they shudder because it was a particularly brutal region during the war.

Through the second year we just existed. It's difficult for me to describe this period beyond the numbness that I felt. Increasingly passive, with no sense of time and no ability to think and rationalize, I became an empty shell;

I don't know how else to put it. There was nothing to motivate us to talk or interact in a meaningful way. Really, what is the difference between one bale of hay and another? One is rounder, one is more square, but it was nothing to talk about. It took too much effort to whisper in order to talk about the nothingness in our lives. We had only the lice and the illnesses. We had tremendous boils, and they were so painful, but after a while we didn't even feel them. It's impossible to describe what cannot be felt, and it takes feelings to be rational. In the beginning, maybe I did feel, but after a while I became accustomed to the situation, perhaps because I was so young. Maybe my parents or my sister could have made the conscious decision to leave the barn and take their chances in the forest. At my young age, what did I know? How could I go out and be able to survive? I just knew there was death outside the barn. There was no one to talk to except those who were in the same situation, so there was no point in talking. If I had seen the children playing, maybe I would have had something to think about or dream about. Other survivors seem to have had more interaction with people than we did. Our life in the barn is similar to that of a prisoner placed into solitary confinement. Prisoners, however, are almost always adults. I was a child. Some years ago, I read a news story about two children who were rescued after being forced to live in a basement. I wonder, how did they turn out? I wish I knew. Recollections of my situation makes me think of the Middle Ages, when people were thrown into dungeons and left to die; perhaps that's a fair comparison. Then again, it's ludicrous for me to compare my experience to anything; it's almost like it's not real. It can't be real, it's not life. But it was—it was my life. Who would have ever predicted only a few years earlier that the circumstances of our lives would lead us to live hidden in a barn for so long? It's impossible to believe that this actually happened to me.

When I tell my story, I get many questions about how I spent my time while in hiding. People ask me if we read books or prayed, or if I became more religious. Their questions suggest an inability to truly conceive what life was like in the hayloft or in the dug-out cavities underneath the floorboards in the ghetto. These days, everyone has so many comforts—most people can't even go a little time without electricity, so how could they possibly understand what it's like to endure two years without washing or what it's like to be frozen with fear, surrounded by darkness and dirt? How could they truly imagine being buried alive even for a short period and then being let out? The movie *Schindler's List* includes a scene in which a child jumps into a sewer to hide and sits there trembling, totally silent, while the *Aktion* is taking place. To read or hear about my story only conveys so much, but to see it makes a different type of impact; I used to refer to that movie a lot because whoever saw it knew exactly what had happened to me, because in that scene, director Steven Spielberg vividly captures something that I myself experienced. Another fine feature film, *The Pianist*, effectively portrays both the intense fear and the unbearable hunger that plagues those who are on the run or in hiding. That element in the movie struck me the most because I know fully what hunger is all about.

Among the themes that I see when I reflect upon my experience hiding in the loft is that of waste and loss, the passage of precious time when my life was truly only beginning. I wish I had been a bird, able to fly in and out, free to see the world outside but then able to return to my family.

I know for sure that if we had remained in hiding for much longer, we would have died in the hayloft. I'm convinced of that.

Liberation

One day in late 1944 or early 1945, the farmer made an unexpected announcement: Russian soldiers were in the area, and my family had to leave the barn at once to join them. I don't remember if my parents argued with the farmer about leaving. We could indeed hear gunfire, and the farmer was afraid of the Russians. I don't specifically remember him coming and saying we had to leave, I just know he carried us down from the loft one by one.

Russian soldiers in battle amid the frozen terrain of Eastern Europe. (Public domain photo.)

At this point we couldn't do much more than crawl on all fours. Our limbs had become atrophied from not moving. Since my father couldn't walk, the farmer brought me down the ladder. He carried me over his shoulder; I couldn't see his face but I remember he was smelly. I tried to stand up and walk but couldn't. The pain felt like rods shooting through my body. Even though it was possible for me to stand up in the loft, I don't ever remember moving to look through the crack—or do much else for that matter—after the first year of our confinement, so when it was time for us to leave, my muscles were too weak to allow me to walk.

We had only the clothes that we wore when we went into hiding, and after two years, they were in horrible shape. Now we were forced out into the cold and snow. Would we survive our time in the loft only to die from exposure? The farmer understandably put us out of the barn at night. Fortunately, we were used to doing nothing unless it was under cover of night, even breathing, it seemed. I don't remember him helping us after that. Maybe he did, but I don't remember it. I do remember crawling in the snow, but I don't know how long or how far we crawled before we reached the Russians; time had no meaning. I know it wasn't days or weeks because the Russian soldiers weren't in full battle yet. What does distance mean when you're crawling through snow and ice without proper clothing? I might have been on rocks or in a field that wasn't plowed. It was terribly cold and my skin stuck to the snow and ice. My hands froze and swelled until my fingers were cracked and oozing; the pain was intense, but it was not a priority at that point. We were just trying to survive. It felt like it took forever to get to the road.

When we finally came to the side of the road, there were many people there, probably other survivors trying to join the Russian soldiers. In those first days after leaving the hayloft, I was petrified by all the people and activity on the road. The Russian trucks were going by so quickly, and there were more and more people coming to the dirt road, perhaps from the forests or out of hiding places. The Russians wouldn't or couldn't take us; I don't know if it was because we were Jews. Local people were also in desperate condition. Soldiers were driving by in whatever vehicle they had and everything was moving quickly. They were in the middle of fighting and didn't have time for us, but I do remember someone on one truck throwing me a blanket and a piece of bread.

TIBUNAL DE Ire INSTANCE
M E T Z

I.F. 77/51

Au nom du Peuple Français

Vu la requête présentée le 17 août 1951, par Mes Caen et Levy,
avocats à Metz pour M. BLITZER Léon, commerçant, 30, rue du Champé
à Metz, requête qui tend à faire déclarer judiciairement le décès de

A N T L E R Malka, dite Mawine

domiciliée à Metz, 30, rue du Champé, déportée en Allemagne
pour motifs politiques et dont on n'a plus signe de vie;

Vu les conclusions de M. le Procureur de la République en date
du 11 octobre 1951-

My Mother's Death

Eventually some of those passing trucks stopped, and the Russian soldiers picked us up. They bandaged my hands, arms, and feet, which were terribly injured from crawling in the freezing snow. The Russians were fighting against the Germans and their sympathizers. We heard the firing of the Katyusha rockets, portable artillery used by the Russians that left a fiery trail as they propelled across the sky. Unless someone has experienced battle firsthand, it is hard to comprehend what it is like.

Background: My mother's passport photo from before she was married. Foreground: The death certificate issued for my mother after the war.

I vividly remember seeing the flashes from the Katyushas in the sky. Maybe those flashes were the reason for an airplane raid on the road that our truck was following, only a few days after we had joined the Russians. We were forced to scramble for safety, and everyone tried to run off the road. I was near my mother; I don't know where my father and sister were.

In the harrowing chaos of the raid, my mother was either shot or hit by a piece of shrapnel; I do not know exactly what happened, but to this day, I can picture the blood running down her side, so much blood. Why did she get hit and I didn't? *Why didn't I scream out?* Maybe because I was numb. Then again, I don't recall hearing my mother scream either. We had just scattered in silence. My eyes locked onto the blood. I don't remember feeling afraid or devastated or anything at all about seeing her wounded.

After the raid was over, the Russians returned and took all of us on one of their trucks to some other place, probably a nearby village; it certainly wasn't the battlefield or the road. They said they would take my mother to an infirmary. My father left my sister and me in a house that had been destroyed and abandoned, and he went with my mother. Soon after he came running back for us; we had to be carried to our mother's bedside because we couldn't walk fast enough. The caregivers at the infirmary spoke Ukrainian, which I understood. My mother was lying on a cot with her hip bandaged. She was covered with lice, as was her bandage and her bed. The picture of the scene in my mind is of one big teeming mound—just like ants on a huge hill—that was my mother covered with lice and vermin. I remember that she was separated from the other patients, most likely because she was a Jewess. I remember the caregivers talking about my mother and referring to her as *Jadova,* which means Jewess in Ukrainian. I understood what they were saying, and that is what has stayed with me my entire life—that she was refused treatment because she was a Jewess. I was angry that she was covered in vermin and no attempt was made to clean her up. In my memory, I see other people lying in their beds not crawling with lice. Why didn't the workers take care of her? Maybe that was common at the time, I don't know. I can only conclude that they just didn't bother with her. At the time, my child's mind quickly realized that she was left to die because of who she was. Don't forget that I knew we were meant to die simply because we were Jewish. Indeed, she was dying, and she knew it. She didn't say anything, and I didn't say anything; I just watched her die. Time had no meaning. I don't know how long it took for her to die, but I can still picture the scene clearly, and it is shattering. Maybe the caregivers wouldn't have been able to save her regardless; then again, maybe she could have survived her injury. If that were the case, I now consider the refusal to treat her as the equivalent of murder.

My father, sister, and I dug a shallow grave with sticks and our hands, and we put her into the ground, wrapped in a blanket, without a casket. I think we had some sort of short service; there were other people standing there with us. We covered her up, and then we got back on the truck. I don't remember us marking the grave at all; Jewish graves weren't really marked in any special way. At most, bodies were buried in plain white boxes meant to disintegrate quickly. But she didn't even have that. In time, I came to realize that she did not have a proper burial. I've seen movies about the early settlers of the United States in which the dead are buried in a shallow grave with just a cross and a prayer, and these depictions are intensely painful to me. Those movies capture a scene similar to my mother's burial, but they cannot begin to convey the pain of my experience, and it is still excruciating to talk about it so many years later.

At the time of my mother's death, I was dead as well on the inside, so to expect that I would be emotional is unrealistic. I simply felt anger at how she was treated, or more accurately, not treated, and later my sister explained her emotions the same way. Suzanne seemed to be even more detached than I was when she talked about our mother's death. Maybe that is the only way we could deal with it. I didn't cry; there were no tears. There should have been, but there were none. There were no tears as we dug the shallow grave and lowered her into it. I don't even remember my father crying. I seem to remember that someone pointed to me and said, "She's not even crying for her mother." I can still see eyes watching my reaction and hear the comments: "Look, the children are not even crying." We were like automatons; there were no emotions because there was just nothing left. We were resigned to the fact that we were meant to die. Until that happened, we were just existing minute to minute, hour to hour.

At the time, I was not angry at whoever caused my mother's death—I was angry at my mother for leaving me. It was difficult to forgive her at the time. I remember experiencing a swelling in my chest, but I can't say it was necessarily because she died. However, I never felt this swelling before or after, except when I remembered her at Yizkor time.

I wish I could have known my mother as she was before the war. I wish I had more memories of her.

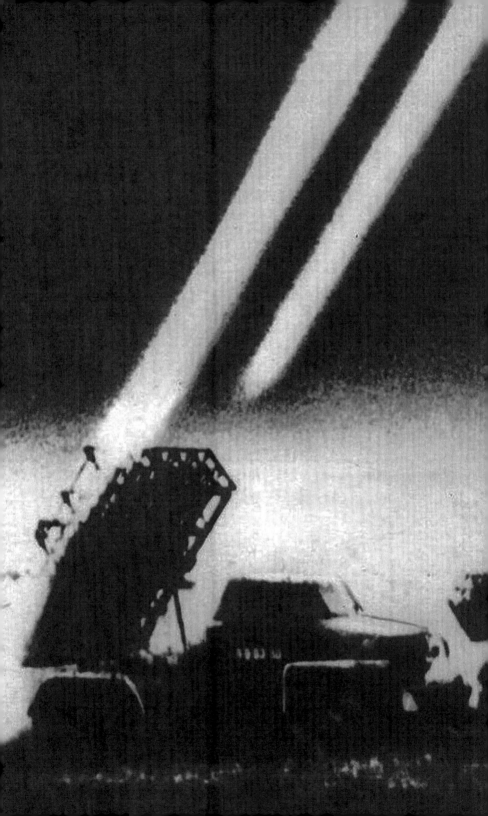

Life with the Russians

After my mother's death, we continued to follow the Russian soldiers. As we approached each village, the peasants fled and the soldiers took over the houses. We became scavengers with the Russians. To me, the Russian soldiers were wonderful! I remember only pleasant things about them, for the most part. Later during the Cold War, many people told me that the Russian soldiers were known to rape and kill, but I did not witness this. Of course these types of incidents happen all the time in war. I remember that everyone was afraid of the Cossacks; they had a reputation of being barbarians, so people feared them more than they did the Russians.

Katyusha rockets streak through the sky after launch. I remember seeing flashes from Katyushas during my time following the Russian soldiers. (Public domain photo.)

My own memories of the Russians are pleasant, or as pleasant as they could be, given the circumstances. I never feared for my life after I was with them, and I grew a little more confident. I didn't know if they were the good guys or the bad guys; to me, they were certainly good.

The soldiers, in fact, were kind enough to tend to me personally. I remember one Russian soldier who held me on his lap while another soldier removed the bandages on my arms and hands. The process was slow and painful because my skin stuck to the bandages, but the soldier rocked me on his lap and sang in my ear, almost in a whisper, trying to make me sing along to distract me from the pain. This is one of the good experiences in my life. The pain was excruciating, but this kind human being did everything he could do to help me. Another time, while one soldier was squeezing out one of my boils, another held me on his lap, humming and swaying to help comfort me. So my memories of the Russian soldiers are positive, because they did their best to try to help me.

Not everything was quite so pleasant for us, of course. I had boils all over my body from the infections created by the lice. I don't know exactly when the boils began to develop, but the biggest one I remember is one that, even after I was in the United States, continued to give me a tingling sensation at the site of the infection. In fact, I can *still* feel it. I remember the pain as my father held me down while a Russian soldier took a knife, sliced that boil open, and started to squeeze. We had no access to medicine that would heal it properly, so the infection just kept

72

coming back. The sanitary conditions were horrid. I'm not sure we washed even after we joined the Russian soldiers. That's why the Red Cross used DDT, a pesticide that is used on mice, to disinfect us. Even the Red Cross didn't have an effective method for dealing with my boils. No one had any real help for us. I specifically remember the Russians walking with rags around their feet because boots and other supplies were scarce. They didn't have anything either, nothing to give us. Everyone was just surviving. People today don't understand this at all.

I remember seeing two people being hanged after the soldiers captured some Germans and local sympathizers. Hanging was the Russians' preferred method of execution for their enemies, and we were right there to watch the public proceedings. The first time I saw it, I almost wanted to help the Russians with their work. Of course, death by hanging is terrible to witness, even more so for a child. Those about to be hung don't submit quietly. They rarely have the courage to stand stoically; rather, they frantically push and fight to get free. Once they are hung, mucus comes out of their nostrils, their tongues stick out, and their mouths gape. The twitching of the bodies was quite ... my point is, why didn't I watch in horror? They were human beings, after all. But I didn't feel pain for them. They were Germans. They represented death to me. In my mind, they had killed my mother. The soldiers didn't make me watch the hangings on purpose. We were just part of the group following the Russian army. It just so happened that we saw the hangings. A child should feel fear and horror after witnessing something like that, and

I didn't. I was almost glad. It's strange, because I talk about not feeling anything, but as I'm thinking about this to tell my story, I *do* have feelings. I don't understand the mixture in myself.

We're interesting, complex beings, we humans; we're not like computers. We're fascinating. We feel things so intensely at some moments, and then again at others we do not. Some people never seem to feel emotion; at this point in my life, I feel sorry for people like that. Personally, I feel privileged to feel all these kinds of emotions, even the negative ones. Is that weird? Perhaps.

After the hangings, the soldiers made bonfires and gathered around the fires to sing and dance the *kozaczka*, the famous dance during which they kick out their legs. The rest of us would join in, and somehow I learned to sing all those songs and to dance. I also remember the Russians talking about the *Komsomol* (a Communist youth group), and I think they tried to indoctrinate us a little bit with their politics.

We were constantly on the move as we trailed the Russians. We followed a primitive dirt road from village to village, never sure what we would encounter next, or when. We scavenged the bombed-out areas we came across along the way, looking for anything we might be able to use to help us feed ourselves. I remember searching through a pile of rubble and discovering a small pot; it was corroded, but I was so proud that I found it! At night we rested in the ditches. Once I saw a Russian soldier making love with a woman inside a destroyed building;

this pleasant memory still makes me smile. Not that I knew exactly what was going on at the time. In fact, I don't *ever* remember seeing my parents hug or trying to be close to one another. They were just surviving.

While we were on the road following the Russians, we met a girl we knew, Esther Grebler. Our family had known Esther and her parents in Monasterzyska, my mother's hometown, and we had been with the Grebler family in some of the ghettos. Esther and my sister were about the same age and had even gone to school together. Esther's parents had been killed, and she was on her own, so my father invited her to join us. In 2007, when I was at a conference in Israel, I was able to reunite with Esther and discuss our various experiences. She was able to validate my memories as well as provide me with new information about my family. I have included Esther's story in another chapter.

As a young girl, I was fluent in Yiddish, Ukrainian, Russian, Polish, and High German; after the war, I also learned French. I am not sure how I learned all these languages. Did I have such a good ear that I easily picked them up? Esther said she and Suzanne went to schools opened by the Russians; perhaps it is through them, as well as the time I spent with the soldiers, that I caught on to the Russian language. Or maybe I learned the Polish and Ukrainian languages from being in the ghettos or just from listening to the Russians. I was also able to read, but I don't remember learning to do so. How I did all this is puzzling to me, and I cannot sort it out.

I don't know precisely how long we followed the Russian army. We stayed with them until they left the region, and we remained in one of the villages. I seem to recall that a truck arrived to take us to the Polish town of Katowice, or maybe it was a train. In Katowice, we were under the care of a Jewish organization working with the Red Cross that helped us clean up and tended to our health needs. Lists with the names of survivors looking to find relatives and friends were on display. I remember my father checking the lists daily, but he never found anyone he knew. Our Katowice address was Wodna 47. Maybe Katowice is where I learned Polish so well. Suzanne and I didn't go out much. I don't recall much about the city, but I remember my father going to different relief organizations looking for help for our family. Sometimes he returned with food and clothing, which was always out of shape and ill-fitting. Still, we were always happy to get whatever we could. No one ever offered to give me toys or anything beyond the bare necessities. Today, we might think to send toys for children along with baskets of food and clothing to those in need, but back then, people did not consider such things, and besides, this was in the aftermath of war. Times were horrible for everybody. I don't ever remember having a doll or any kind of toy as a child, although my sister remembered having a doll before the war. Given our circumstances after the war, however, to think of toys would have been frivolous.

I don't remember anyone saying specifically that the war was over; however, to me, it didn't matter, because my fears and sadness were not over. During our years in hiding and in the time immediately following, I really didn't know that a war of such an immense scale was going on. I never knew of Auschwitz or any of the other aspects of World War II that I've learned about in the last thirty years. I didn't know of the other events happening in the world at the time. It is as if I existed in suspension from reality during the years of the war and immediately after.

We were in Katowice for a while, although I'm not sure exactly how long; my sister said we were then sent to some sort of rehabilitation camp in Prague, Czechoslovakia, before we returned to France sometime near the end of 1946. I don't know which organization made the arrangements for us to go back to France, but we were sent to Paris on a military plane that was hollow on the inside; we flew sitting on the floor.

Returning to Metz

I was about eleven years old when we returned to France. Once we arrived in Paris, we were forced to go through the delousing process all over again; apparently the treatments in Katowice hadn't done the job. We were made to shed all our clothing, and our bodies were shaved and sprayed with DDT to be sure we had no lice or vermin. I remember how ashamed and degraded I felt. I was treated like an animal, told to turn this way, to do this, to do that. The workers used a canister with a hand pump to spray us; I covered my face with my hands. Nobody made any attempt to be nice to us or to explain the process.

Upper left: My father in front of our apartment in Metz in about 1948. Center: Herb and I during a visit to Metz in 2004, on the same street where my father stood in the photo above.

The workers instead made demands in stern voices, and I didn't understand most of what they said because they spoke in French, a language I did not yet know. We were held in one building until all of the lice and other vermin were gone, perhaps as long as a month, so that we would be sure not to contaminate anyone else.

The food we were given while we were in Paris was very rich. I remember being fed chunks of butter and horse meat as well as brains to make me stronger; I was also made to suck out the marrow from bones for the extra nourishment and vitamins. I think a local Jewish organization supported by the Americans was feeding us, but the food they gave us was so strange. The idea of eating brains was especially mind-boggling to me at the time, but I understand now that brains were often fed to people as a delicacy.

We were given packages of donated clothing, some of it torn and worn out. It's amazing to me that charities today want everything donated to be in good condition, cleaned and on a hanger. After the war, we were lucky to get even torn pieces of clothing. People had to make something out of nothing.

Health workers continued to tend to my boils and other injuries, but I wasn't really healed for several years, until I was about sixteen. Some of my injuries were still not completely healed when I came to the United States; my skin would still split in the winter time, especially my hands and feet. For many years, I felt like I still had these injuries, even after they were healed and no longer there.

Arrangements were finally made for us to go back to Metz on a train from Paris. By this time, my Aunt Cella was back with her family in Metz. They had returned from Switzerland, where they fled for safety during the war and had been interned in a camp for Jews. Initially they had gone to the south of France, but later, as conditions worsened, they traveled over the mountains by foot to get to Switzerland. It's a fascinating story unto itself; in fact, my cousin Henri Kanter wrote a book, *Mémoires... Mémoire*, about their experiences during the war.

My aunt never asked how my mother died. No one wanted to hear about our experiences, and I did not want to talk about them either. I tried hard to forget how I saw my mother just before she died, but the sadness did not leave me for a long time. I do not remember any happy moments in this era. I was obsessed with my mother. It seems terrible not to have any wonderful memories of my mother, no warm, bonding moments that can be cherished. Only on a visit to France in January 1999 did I finally tell my aunt's children how my mother died. I had the sense that they did not really want to hear the details; they turned their heads away and didn't make eye contact with me. My aunt was dead by then, and she never knew the truth. She didn't want to know.

Metz was militarily important because it is near the borders of Germany, Belgium, Luxembourg, and Switzerland. Because of its strategic location, different countries fought for control over the city through the centuries, and its nationality went back and forth. In fact, at one time it was a walled city, in an effort to try to protect itself. Today, all that remains of the wall are ancient entrances. In World War I, my husband's stepfather, an American soldier, was wounded in Metz. We still have the Purple Heart medal he received. I never really saw much of Metz until the mid-1990s, when my cousin drove me around to see the sights. Immediately after the war, however, we had no car or means to travel.

After World War II ended, American troops were stationed in Metz, and unfortunately, they were very poorly behaved. Looking back now, it was like a scene from *The Ugly American*. The victorious Americans acted as if everything belonged to them. They chased all the girls, and they were loud at a time when Europeans spoke softly and were conservative. They were also taller than the local people, so they stood apart even more. American soldiers had more provisions and earned more money than the French soldiers, so they could also pay more for their lodging or anything else they wanted. This resulted in considerable unrest in the town. The French people were stupidly proud; they owed a big debt to the United States, but they didn't like the American troops and resented them tremendously. In my own apartment building, there were children fathered by Americans who didn't marry the mothers. Nonetheless, I do have some pleasant memories of Americans from that time. I remember going with someone to an event featuring the Harlem Globetrotters. We didn't have the money for a ticket, so we climbed a fence to see the show. At the time, I thought they were just incredible. It was mind-boggling to me. They were great.

After our initial time in Metz, my aunt helped us rent a flat in 32 Rue des Allmand. That is where my second life really begins. My father, sister, and I moved into the apartment along with Esther, although she was soon sent to Israel to be with family. My father looked unsuccessfully for work and finally resumed the kind of business he did before the war, peddling clothing, bedding, and other items to people who lived in the nearby villages. A wholesale house provided him with items to sell on credit, and he in turn allowed the villagers to buy items on credit. As the villagers repaid my father little by little, he could then repay the wholesale house. Unfortunately, many of the farmers either didn't pay him or just made minimal payments, making it hard for my father to earn any money for himself. The local iron factory eventually closed, making times hard for everyone in the area.

Suzanne and I did finishing work, such as sewing buttons on garments, for Bernard Spiegelmann, a custom tailor. At that time, everyone bought their clothing from a tailor. I became an expert at making the many buttonholes in a pair of pants. My father also learned how to sew and began making pants, but the work was not steady for him, so I presume he wasn't very neat. I cleaned our apartment during the day and sewed at night. Suzanne was a young woman, beautiful, and she was going out a lot with friends. My cousins were also her age, so I imagine they went in groups to various places while I stayed at home to take care of things.

Papa was a difficult man. He was handsome, with dark hair, flashing eyes, and high cheekbones. He attracted many women. The widow of the wholesaler from whom my father got his dry goods to sell wanted to marry Papa, but she wasn't attractive enough for him. He had a quick temper and was extremely hyper and nervous like my sister. He was a philanderer, so I can only imagine the misery this caused for my mother before the war. My Aunt Cella and her husband had a lot of disdain for my father. He knew this, and so did Suzanne and I. Plus, he was not successful in making a living for himself or his children. The knowledge that so many people did not like or respect our father weighed heavily on my sister and me. In those days, I was mad at him for failing us; now I see him as simply a very unhappy human being, a broken man.

Our apartment had two tiny rooms and a small kitchen. A table covered with a plastic cloth stood near a coal stove. Coal had to be brought up three flights of stairs to the apartment to heat the stove for cooking. A sewing machine on a stand was placed nearby. Each floor of the building had one common bathroom. The Rigleviche family lived in one of the first floor apartments: father, mother, and an extremely handsome son. On the second floor was a pretty blue-eyed prostitute who had several children with some American GIs. She thought one of the soldiers might take her to the United States, but that never happened. I know there were other neighbors, but

they are mostly faceless; they kept to themselves and did-
n't interact with me. Cats were always around; one huge
black cat in particular petrified me. One night it jumped
on me when I went up the stairway from the bathroom.
The whole building was always dark and unfriendly; I
hated it.

My Aunt Cella taught me to perform many everyday
tasks. Preparation for a Friday night chicken dinner began
with a visit to the butcher with my aunt and sister. We
inspected the chickens to be sure that they had the right
amount of fat near their anus and blew through the feathers to see how fat they were. We took our selection to the
kosher butcher, who then tied the chicken's legs, said a
prayer, and slit its throat, hanging it upside down to let
the blood flow out. The bird twitched for a while and then
hung limp. I don't remember feeling very much at the
sight. The butcher wrapped the chicken in paper to be
taken home. There I doused the chicken with boiled
water and plucked the feathers off it until the bird was
clean, taking care not to harm the spleen and gall. I then
went through the process of making it kosher, soaking it
in water for an hour, then putting salt all over it. My aunt
also taught me how to mix flour, water, eggs, and yeast to
make challah. I kneaded the dough in a large bowl, over
and over, and then gave it a pat to see if it was soft enough.
I covered it for an hour or two so it would rise. Then I cut
the dough into three pieces, pinched it out, rolled it out,
and braided it to make a loaf of bread to bake. To make
noodles, I used the same process without the yeast, but
with a pinch of salt and sugar to keep the dough moist. I

cut the dough into pieces, rolled it out flat with a glass to make it very thin, sprinkled flour over it every time, and then lifted and rolled it some more. Then I let the dough dry before I folded it to make a roll and cut the size noodle I wanted. This was all the ritual preparation for the Friday night dinner. Carp was the first course, then chicken soup, the challah, and the boiled chicken. Carp was the only kind of fish available or desirable at the time. I kept the carp in water until I was ready to smash its head. When it stopped moving, I slit the belly and took out the intestines, and then I took out the eyes and scraped off the scales. I added salt and sugar in the cooking. The head was always reserved for Papa out of respect for him.

Another dish I learned to make was galla. I took the hooves from a cow, boiled them to remove the hair, stripped the skin off the hoof, and then boiled what was left with salt and lots of garlic, to be served cold the next day with mustard and bread. It was the original Jello. I also learned to make *kishka*, which is a sausage made with chicken stuffed into beef intestines. The development of my cooking skills showed a large contrast from what I ate during my first year in Metz, when I was served horse meat because it was thought to have special nutrients that I supposedly needed.

During Passover, a religious man, likely someone from the synagogue, came to our home and watched as I koshered the pots, dishes, and stove. Most Jewish families had someone come in to certify that their house was truly kosher. Jews are forbidden to eat leavened bread or any kind of grain during Passover, so I scrubbed not only the kitchen, but all the rooms in the house; I had to be sure there was not a crumb anywhere. I boiled water in a large pot for a certain amount of time, added my small pots, and then blanched the dishes. Silverware had to be buried for a certain length of time in dirt. Curtains were washed. The stove had to have red hot coals totally covering the top. Then the kitchen was ready for Pesach (Passover). I was only twelve years old, but I did all these things, even if I wasn't the best of housekeepers. Even now, in the Orthodox tradition, getting ready for Passover is still quite strenuous; some families even have two kitchens, one only used for Pesach. I still follow some traditions but not all; it makes me feel good to do so. Today, it sounds like just a good cleaning of the house, but really it was much more than that; it was a religious ritual. These things must be done. Between the cooking, cleaning, sewing, and lugging coal up the stairs, I was kept busy!

Across the street was a little grocery market where I frequently asked to buy on credit. I was always hungry in those days; I cannot tell you how hungry I used to be. I often cried to my father over our circumstances; I was beginning to dislike him for not being able to provide for us. I feel terrible for treating my father that way when he probably couldn't do anything to change our situation. He was also proud. We just seemed to be lost in the city, and even the Jewish organizations and the Jewish community didn't help us.

29e Année
N° 10

LE NOUVEAU CERTIFICAT D'ÉTUDES PRIMAIRES & les BOURSES

1er Juillet
1947

Organe de préparation.
Honoré d'une souscription du Conseil municipal de Paris et du Conseil général de la Seine
pour un service d'abonnement à toutes les Écoles primaires publiques de Paris et du Département.
Paraît le 1er de chaque mois.
France, un an : 60 fr. — **Étranger**, un an : 75 fr.
Administration et Rédaction : LIBRAIRIE DELAGRAVE, 15, rue Soufflot, PARIS, Ve.
C. C. P. PARIS 207-55

Fondateur	Directeur
M. J.-B. TARTIÈRE	M. CHAPUIS
Inspecteur Hre de l'Enseignement Primaire de la Seine	Inspecteur Hre de l'Enseignement Primaire de la Seine

AVANT DE NOUS METTRE EN TRAIN

SIMPLES PROPOS

Vous ne trouverez plus dans ce numéro, chers lecteurs, la préparation au Certificat (1re partie), l'examen étant supprimé. Toutefois nous avons cru devoir conserver les textes et les développements qui se rattachaient à cette préparation et qui s'adressaient surtout aux élèves du cours moyen. Vous les trouverez dans la seconde moitié du numéro, *sous le titre : Pour le cours moyen*.

Les nombreuses copies reçues au cours de cette année scolaire par notre Comité de correction, les progrès nets et rapides qu'elles nous ont révélés nous amènent à penser que ces textes vous apportaient une aide utile. Mais l'an prochain nous devrons nécessairement réserver une place à la préparation de l'examen d'admission en première année des cours complémentaires et à celle du Concours d'entrée en sixième secondaire, qui parfois seront d'un niveau légèrement plus élevé que celui de l'examen remplacé. Quelles solutions nous proposez-vous ? Exprimez-nous vos désirs en nous envoyant des textes. Nous retiendrons, cela va de soi, la solution qui réunira le plus de suffrages.

Si l'année scolaire qui se termine ne nous a pas encore apporté l'organisation définitive du Certificat d'études, comme nous en exprimions le désir l'an dernier, elle nous a procuré des satisfactions d'un autre ordre qui sont pour nous de précieux encouragements.

Tout d'abord, nous avons retrouvé nos anciens abonnés du Nord et du Nord-Est qui, pendant quatre longues années, ont été complètement séparés de nous. En nous communiquant les textes de cette année, ils nous font part des succès brillants obtenus par leurs élèves. Nous les en félicitons bien cordialement. Si comme ils ont l'amabilité de nous l'écrire, en termes particulièrement touchants, l'action du « Nouveau Certificat d'études » n'est pas étrangère à ces résultats, nous en sommes très heureux. Nous songeons plus encore tout à la valeur éprouvée des maîtres en même temps qu'ils attestent la solidarité étroite unissant le journal à ses aimables lecteurs.

L'œuvre commune ne se limite pas à la Métropole, elle s'étend à tous les pays de l'Union française. Vous avez pu lire dans nos derniers numéros des textes envoyés de très loin et souvent par avion, comme d'ailleurs des copies adressées à notre comité de correction. Les distances n'existent plus. Que nos aimables correspondants trouvent ici l'expression de notre vive reconnaissance.

Nous ne voulons pas laisser se terminer cette année scolaire sans souhaiter à nos lecteurs, maîtres, parents et élèves, d'excellentes vacances. Et nous ajoutons : « A la rentrée d'octobre ».

LE CERTIFICAT D'ÉTUDES PRIMAIRES EN 1946 (Ancien régime)

EXAMEN N° 1

(Les corrigés de cet examen seront donnés dans le n° 11).

I. — Rédaction (Franche-Comté.)

Les soirs d'été, on prend le frais assez tard. Décrivez l'aspect du village — ou de votre quartier — quand vient la nuit en cette saison : les allées et venues, les conversations sur le pas des portes, les bruits qui s'éteignent peu à peu.

II. — Dictée (Franche-Comté.)

SÉCHERESSE. — Un été superbement bleu brûla la terre. Le printemps ayant été frais, les labours de mars avaient fait dans les champs d'argile de grosses mottes luisantes ; elles devinrent si dures par la suite, ces mottes, qu'on les aurait prises pour d'énormes briques. Les gens s'en désolaient, ils guettaient les nuages, sondaient l'horizon pâle, suivaient de l'œil la moindre fumée. Deux ou trois fois, des flocons très hauts et très blancs, semblables à de la laine bien cardée, cachèrent le soleil... Mais la belle nuée s'en allait doucement comme une lente troupe d'oiseaux sauvages, et bientôt on la voyait massée en un tout petit coin du ciel.

PÉROCHON.

QUESTIONS. — 1° Donnez le sens des expressions : *sondaient l'horizon, suivaient de l'œil, laine cardée.*

2° Relevez la comparaison contenue dans la dernière phrase et dites si elle est juste.

3° Conjuguez *s'en aller* à la 3e personne du singulier des temps simples de l'indicatif.

III. — Calcul (Franche-Comté.)

a. — QUESTIONS. — 1° Une citerne un carré de 2 m de côté. A quelle l'eau quand elle en contient 6 000

Going to School

After the war, I was very withdrawn, and I did not speak much, maybe because I was frightened or in too much pain. I'm not sure how long this lasted, but it's as though I were two people, one trying to survive and the other one who was traumatized. This made things very difficult for me when I was finally enrolled in the local school, at age eleven or twelve. I could read by then, so at some point I must have taught myself to do so. I knew how to read Russian (which is difficult), German (I can do basic reading today), and Polish.

Left: A copy of the first test I took at a small Jewish school in 1947. Upper right: Me at about age 12 in France.

I even knew how to read a little Yiddish at one time. Still, I was put into the first grade because I had never been to a "real" school and didn't have any formal learning. In addition, my appearance was horrible; I had boils all over my body that were hidden by unflattering clothes that I hated.

My hair was shaved around the large boil on my head, and I tried to arrange my remaining hair over the bald spot. I can still feel it to this day. I was taller than most; I was an oddity. No one wanted to be near me in the school courtyard at recess. Back then, teachers didn't seem to do anything to help when they saw an isolated child. The kids sensed I was different, and they made fun of me, but I didn't know a word of French at the time. I still remember them laughing at me and taunting me, but I didn't understand. They called me *sale juive* ("dirty Jew"). When I learned what they were saying, I lost control of my bladder, my same old problem and reaction to fear. I remember the other children pointing and laughing at me as the urine ran down my legs. However, I didn't cry, just as I didn't cry when other traumatic experiences happened to me during my childhood. For a long time, I had problems with bladder control at night. Mind you, we didn't have a washing machine; we had to take big items to a place where there were common washing facilities with large wash tubs and scrubbing boards. My lack of bladder control was a real problem.

My father or aunt decided to take me out of the local school in favor of a small Jewish school in which each student in the class was taught differently according to individual needs. The school was far away, and I had to walk there with my cousins who lived a couple of streets away from us. I still remember the faces of some of the other school kids. My teacher, Monsieur Lang, was an old-school German Jewish teacher, and he smacked students who didn't obey. He was bald and rotund and totally intimidating to me. I was left-handed, and Monsieur Lang tried to make me right-handed. He had a long stick made out of soft bamboo that he used to hit my hands, eventually breaking open wounds that had finally begun to heal.

I failed my first test at my new school; I still have the report card! It was very shameful to me, and I never went back. I was between twelve and thirteen years old at the time. My family decided to send me to ORT, a school in Strasbourg that taught vocational skills, and I was to learn sewing. I think my aunt helped to get me into the school. My cousin Henri Kanter took me to Strasbourg on the train and paid for my ticket. This was the second ORT school established after the war. Years later, I wrote to the school requesting to have my records sent to me, but they were in storage and apparently too difficult to retrieve.

At ORT, it was possible to learn all aspects of being a seamstress. The school offered classes in clothing design and pattern-making. I was at ORT for maybe a full scholastic year, but I was frequently hospitalized because of my poor health. I had kidney problems and was constantly ill. I think it took most students two or three years to complete the program at ORT, but I dropped out because I wasn't doing well. I really needed a one-on-one tutor, and this was never available to me. Eventually, I was asked to leave. Later, when I married, my father bought me a sewing machine, and I made clothes, coats, and dresses for myself and everyone around me. I could look at magazines and copy the clothes and styles. Despite these skills, I ultimately had very little formal schooling. My unsuccessful attempts at the local school, the Jewish school, and ORT made me feel like a failure. After I came to the United States and was married, I tried to go to high school. I had a lot of knowledge, but the classes had no relevance to my life, and I was not successful. I actually wanted to be tested in order to be given a high-school diploma without taking all the classes, but I was not allowed. I've since taken courses at Wayne State University in Detroit, and I did quite well, so I am obviously not dumb. After my children went to school, I passed various tests, including my real-estate exams, with flying colors, so I think if I had been given the chance to take a high-school equivalency exam, I would have passed. I was crushed when I wasn't allowed to take the test. My confidence was destroyed, and I just gave up. I would have been required to start with grade one and get a certificate for each grade. Who had the time for that?

My Sister's Marriage

Suzanne was married very soon after our return to Metz, to Bernard Spiegelmann, the tailor for whom we worked. She wore a white gown that was borrowed, and the wedding was in a little hall. Although there was a Jewish community in Metz, Bernard did not want to have a Jewish ceremony, but my father, aunt, and everybody else insisted on it. Everyone brought a dish to eat, something people usually did for a poor girl whose parents could not afford a nice party. I know how degrading that must have been for her.

Suzanne and Bernard Spiegelmann on their wedding day in May 1947.

Suzanne's wedding day was not a happy one for other reasons, as well: she was actually in love with someone else. I don't know if she ever talked to my father about her feelings, but I think he probably knew she didn't want to marry Bernard. I remember her crying on the way to her wedding ceremony. She said that she didn't want to get married, but she wasn't strong enough to resist the pressures of what others thought was best for her. A person who has lived so many years with nothing can have a hard time taking control of her own life. Families used to control their children much more in those years. In Paris, maybe it would have been different, I don't know, but in Metz, there was no way out. In Metz, we were at the bottom of the heap of the Jewish community. The community didn't respect my father, so they didn't respect us. Dowry was very important, and even though she was beautiful, my sister didn't have anything except one or two suits on her back, and this limited her marriage options. After her wedding, Suzanne withdrew into herself. Bernard may not have been the best person for someone who had such a traumatized life, even though he really loved Suzanne. He was a man for whom there was just black and white, no gray. Suzanne needed someone who would understand her better.

After the marriage, Suzanne and Bernard moved into a small apartment. He molded her into the person she became. Raised Orthodox, Bernard joined the French Resistance during the war. He was a decorated fighter, and he was imprisoned for a time in Italy. These experiences led him to reject his heritage and join the Communist Party.

Suzanne embraced Bernard's political philosophies, which caused both of them to be shunned by the local Jewish community. However, over time, they had different values about what was important. Although both Bernard and Suzanne were satisfied with a simple life early on and were committed to providing a foremost education to their children, Suzanne eventually wanted more of what the world had to offer, and she became focused on her family's material security as well. This difference in values created friction between her and Bernard.

As my father saw it, Bernard had a business and could support Suzanne. As it turned out, however, the business really belonged to his two young nephews, who were in an orphanage because their parents had died in the war. My father didn't know Bernard was just holding onto to the business for the boys. Within a few months after her marriage began, my sister had to assume responsibility for raising these two children.

Sylvan Roth, another of Bernard's nephews, lived with my brother-in-law and was very close to him because all of his other family members had been murdered during the war. A teen when Bernard and Suzanne married, he resented my sister because he thought she took Bernard away from him. Sylvan was a gorgeous young man. He became active in the Jewish youth group because he wanted to go to Israel. I remember being in love with him; he was so tall and handsome! He sometimes took children, including me, to the park, where we would walk with him. I remember once we came to a stream, and the older girls said that they could not cross the stream because they had their periods, so he carried them across, one by one. I pretended I had mine too so he would take me in his arms and carry me across. About forty years later, Sylvan had a job in New York, and my husband and I went to see him; I invited him to come to our hotel and meet us. We went to the lobby and looked around, but all I saw was this bald little man walking around with a bunch of flowers, looking for someone. My husband approached him, and sure enough, it was Sylvan! What a disappointment! Still, he was the sweetest man in the world. Unfortunately, he passed away recently. His son lives in Ann Arbor, Michigan, and I once told him the story about his father carrying me across the stream. I had told Sylvan the story earlier, but of course, he didn't remember everything I did and didn't see himself as a handsome, tall, young man that the girls swooned over!

Memories from Our Life in France

Life in France continued to be extremely hard for us. At one point, my father wrote to his brother in America, asking for a suit of clothes so that he could dress better in the hope that people wouldn't despise him so much. It was a very poignant letter; he wrote about wanting to look human and presentable so people wouldn't look at him in the same disdainful way.

Background: A portion of a letter my father wrote to his brother in America. Upper right: Me, my father, and Suzanne in early 1947.

His description of himself matched how I felt about my own appearance. In the letter, when my father described some of our experiences, he used the word *Malhouma* for the Holocaust, meaning "the destruction" in Yiddish. This term sounds more significant to me than the word Holocaust; I always thought Holocaust was too inadequate to describe what happened. Later in my life, I got mad at my psychiatrist for using the word Holocaust.

I had a couple of girlfriends during this time, but I was certainly never part of the "in" crowd. Even at the age of thirteen, because of my awkward looks and terrible clothing, I felt I was the least attractive person in our little group. Furthermore, my father was very strict. In my teens, if I were to sneak out of the house and go walking on the main street with other girls, just innocently talking and laughing, my father would lock the door and not let me in when I returned home. I had to pound and pound for a long time at night before he would let me in. He would be very angry with me for staying out. Still, I have to say that he loved me and probably would have killed for me.

To earn some money in Metz, I sometimes went to a local art performance building to sing Russian songs and dance the *kozaczka*. I don't remember being paid very much, however. In the late 1990s when I visited Metz, my cousin showed me the building, and I had flashbacks of these memories.

Since I was still recovering from my wartime experiences, I was sent on two occasions to a farm where I could receive better nutrition. I enjoyed staying with the couple who owned the farm, and my health did improve somewhat. At one point, I was sent to live with my Aunt Regina, one of my mother's sisters, who was married and living in the Paris suburb of Argenteuil. She and her husband wanted to adopt me, and my father was in agreement with this plan. I didn't like my uncle, however; he was much younger than my aunt, and I think he married her because she was a seamstress and had accumulated a little money. She was very meek. I think he wanted to take me in because he thought I could be her assistant in their women's clothing store, handling customers while my aunt stayed in the back. He was trying to teach me the business, he said, and several times he introduced me to various people, but I thought he was too "touchy." I might have been about fifteen at this time, and Suzanne was already married. I was mad at my father for even thinking he would let someone else adopt me, although I know now the real reason was because he couldn't feed me. Eventually, I left my aunt and went to the Jewish orphanage where Bernard's two nephews were staying. I begged them to give me enough money to take the train back to Metz, which they did. I think my father was secretly glad that I came back. I'm so sorry for some of the little grudges I held against him. Even if I had wanted someone to adopt me, I couldn't have left my father. I felt responsible for him, and my conscience never would have let me leave him.

When my father was ill with pneumonia or other respiratory problems, he had me administer a treatment called *bahnkes* (also known as cupping) that was used to treat the sick. I became a specialist in *bahnkes* because it was the only medical treatment available to us. A small glass specially curved with a large rounded rim was used. First, I swabbed the inside of the glass and my father's chest or back with alcohol. I then used a match to light the alcohol fumes inside the glass and quickly put it on his skin, forming suction and a vacuum. The treatment was supposed to take out the brunt of the illness, sort of like leeches were used in the past. The flame extinguished rapidly with no air, and the skin swelled up underneath, usually turning black. The blacker the skin became, the more severe the illness. If a person receiving the treatment wasn't sick, the skin would not turn black; it's really strange how it worked. I put my fingernail between the glass and the skin and the glass popped off. I then disinfected the bubbles of raised skin with alcohol. The process wasn't painful, but I had to be quick to be sure not to burn the skin. I was an expert. Cupping was a commonly accepted treatment for a wide range of illnesses. We even brought a set of these glasses to the United States, and I used them for a number of years; that's how my father would want to be treated whenever he was sick. I didn't keep these glasses, but I wish I had.

For all practical purposes, I had become the head of our family, but it should have been the reverse. Even though I was a child, I was never a child; my childhood had been stolen from me, and I had become an adult in a child's body.

Coming to the United States

My father decided that there no future for him in France and that he wanted a new life; he wanted to go somewhere where he could start over. He chose the United States because he had a brother and a sister there. Both my Uncle Louis in New York and my Aunt Helen in Detroit were Kroliks, which was my father's original surname. My father's request to emigrate to the U.S. was not immediately granted because he was not a French citizen; he was just a Polish citizen residing in France. The U.S. had quotas restricting the number of citizens from each country who could enter, and we had to wait until there was an opening for a Polish citizen.

Left: The Samaria, *the ship that brought me to the United States in 1953. Right: Me on the deck of the* Samaria *during my voyage across the Atlantic.*

I was born in France, so I was a French citizen and could have come to the United States sooner than my father, but of course I wanted to wait until we could both go together. He would have been lost without me, or at least I thought. He wanted Suzanne to come with us, but she was married, so naturally she wouldn't come. If he could have made a living in Metz, I think we would have stayed, but he just couldn't support us there. He wasn't doing very well, emotionally or financially. He was also drinking. I too wanted a new and better life, and I could see that nothing was happening in France. I wanted to go to Israel, which was the thing to do in those days for young people. The thought of going to Israel was very exciting to me. I told my father he would have to change his lifestyle if he wanted me to go with him to the United States; otherwise I was going to Israel. He did stop drinking, so here I am.

Of course, all our documentation had been destroyed in the war. He collected all the necessary replacement paperwork by himself, going to the various offices, filing claims, making depositions before judges, and tending to many other details so that our documents could be reissued. In 1953, he finally got his immigration papers, and we boarded the Cunard ship *Samaria* in Cherbourg to leave for the United States. I still have the menu from the ship with all the signatures from the passengers at our table. I was very sick on the voyage, and everyone was so kind to me. Today, my husband and I have a sailboat; how I can sail after the experience of crossing the Atlantic, I don't know! I believe the voyage to the United States took seven to ten days. We arrived in February 1953, and my Uncle Louis picked us up at the port. I can't remember going through customs, maybe because I was stressed or fearful. I was not a very worldly person and not used to traveling.

New York was so overwhelming to us. We went to live in my uncle's one-bedroom apartment on Pitkin Avenue in Brooklyn. There was hardly any room. We stayed there for a short while, maybe a few weeks. My Uncle Louis worked in a laundry, and he tried to find jobs for us. Then my Aunt Helen from Detroit came to discuss where we should live. She decided that she didn't want us to come to Detroit, and she fought with my father and uncle something fierce about where we should live. I think she was afraid of the burden we might impose on her. In 1939, Aunt Helen had taken in her brother's son and daughter, my cousins Max and Rosa, when they became orphaned, and they stayed with her for a number of years during the war. It was a very unhappy experience; I believe they were emotionally damaged by her treatment of them. Max moved out from her house when he was thirteen years old; one of his professors knew his troubles and gave or rented him a room. Rosa had to stay because she was younger. She is still extremely angry about this time in her life, and to this day doesn't speak to our cousin Alvin, Aunt Helen's son. Perhaps Aunt Helen thought my father and I would be a burden like my cousins had been. However, she finally but grudgingly acquiesced and consented to take us back to Detroit.

Life in Detroit

I remember traveling by train to Detroit and then arriving at my Aunt Helen's house. She lived on Snowden Avenue, in an upper-middle-class area in the city. Her husband was a roofing contractor, and he made a decent living. She was one of those people who watched every penny, buying overripe fruit and vegetables to save money. She was extremely frugal, but when she died, she left a very nice inheritance to her two children. Like my sister, my Aunt Helen denied herself just about everything.

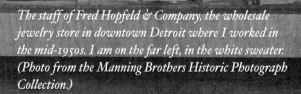

The staff of Fred Hopfeld & Company, the wholesale jewelry store in downtown Detroit where I worked in the mid-1950s. I am on the far left, in the white sweater. (Photo from the Manning Brothers Historic Photograph Collection.)

My aunt and uncle didn't ask us any questions about the war; they didn't want to talk about it. In fact, no one asked us about the war or our experiences, and we didn't want to talk about them, either. Many years prior in France, we had made the conscious decision not to dwell on the past. People in the United States were just like the people in France: no one wanted to know anything. We pushed it into the back of our minds. We chose to make a new life instead of living in the past. This was a new way of survival.

Before we came to the United States, my aunt thought that it would be a good idea if I registered my age on my passport and other official documents as a year or two younger than it actually was. Why? So I would be more eligible for marriage. I was almost nineteen, and she thought that if I were younger, I'd have more of a chance to catch a husband. She was afraid my marriage chances were limited because I was a poor girl. I refused to lie about my age, however, and as it turned out, I had oodles of suitors after me!

My two cousins lived at home with us, Estelle and Alvin Ring. Estelle was a sweet girl of about fourteen years of age; Alvin was a couple of years older than I was, and he was extremely shy. I was a terrible influence on him, or so my aunt thought. I went to night-school classes to learn to speak English. I was a quick study, and Alvin helped me practice the language. He was very kind. He was in medical school, and he took me to the fraternity dances, since he didn't have a girlfriend. My aunt took me to the bargain basement of Hudson's department store to buy me a dress to wear to formal dances. I really hated that dress! I was just trying to get acclimated in the beginning, and Alvin was so kind to me that my aunt was afraid we would fall in love. Of course, that never even occurred to us; we were just friends and cousins.

Although I spoke a number of languages when I came to the United States, I just wanted to be an American. I worked very hard to learn English in my night-school classes, and I didn't want to dwell on any other language. Other students exchanged words in Polish and Ukrainian, but this made me cringe because I wanted so much to forget the past and become totally involved with my new life in a free country. Still, people called us "greenies" because we were the green ones, the newcomers.

My father still needed a lot of medical care. My aunt took him to Sinai hospital, which was especially kind to the new immigrants, providing free or reduced-cost care; she would never pay to take my father to a private physician who would charge more. My father also had many dental problems. He needed to have teeth pulled and bridges made. Implants were not common in the United States at the time, even though people in France were getting them. My aunt would have had to pay for the bridges, and she decided it was too expensive. Instead, a dentist pulled all my father's teeth and gave him some ill-fitting false teeth. He was never able to adapt to them, and he was resentful of her because of this. I never had dental care until I came to the United States. My aunt wasn't willing to take me to a "real" dentist; my cousin Alvin had a friend who was in dental school, and I had my first dental cleaning in his home. After Herb and I were married, he took me to his dentist, and that was when I began to get proper dental care. I needed a lot of work! Herb said he should have examined my teeth before marrying me like someone would do to a horse before buying it!

Living with my aunt became difficult because I knew she resented us being there. When I overheard her talking in Yiddish to some of her friends, relating to them what a burden we were, I told my father we needed to leave and find our own place to live.

My father was still quite handsome at the time, and many ladies liked him. An acquaintance of my aunt, who had a daughter a little older than me, offered to let us stay with them in their two-bedroom apartment. The lady and her daughter stayed in one bedroom, while my father and I shared the other room and its lone bed. That she took us in when she had such a tiny apartment means more than I can describe. Rarely did anyone go to such an extreme for us. She helped to find my father a job in a Chinese laundry, but because he didn't yet speak English, it was very hard for him. She also helped me get a job in downtown Detroit doing piecework at a blouse factory. It was essentially a sweatshop, and I was paid not by the hour, but for each item I completed. I was probably the youngest and least experienced of the workers and not very fast, so I didn't make enough to support us. Then one day someone in the building saw me in the elevator and asked if I would model, so I quit the sweatshop and modeled blouses for a wholesaler. I was paid minimum wages, of course. After that, I had a similar job modeling furs and then worked as a stockperson in a wholesale custom jewelry store, Fred Hopfeld & Company. I worked hard there, and I could remember the stock numbers of thousands of pieces of jewelry that were in small packets. The Hopfelds were also immigrants, German Jews, and had one daughter, Helga, who I still see on occasion. All the jobs were in the same building in downtown Detroit, just on different floors.

At the apartment, some conflicts began to develop. I had blossomed in many ways; I became more outgoing and was physically attractive. Not that I was that pretty. My face was just pleasant, but I had a good figure. One time before I was married I was walking in New York during a visit with relatives, and I was stopped by some men who were driving by in a convertible and asked if I wanted to be represented by a modeling agency. My newfound confidence and looks were not appreciated by everyone, however. Our landlady's daughter had an eye on her cousin, hoping he would marry her, but he was beginning to come around the apartment too often; they may have been afraid it was because of me. I don't know if we were asked to leave or if we did so on our own, but around 1954 or 1955 we decided to rent a room from another woman who allowed us to stay in the bedroom of her son, who was in the army. We were able to pay the rent on what we were earning, so it was a good move.

Around the same time that we moved, my father applied for a job at Ford Motor Company. He lied about his age because companies were reluctant to hire older workers. He was hired in at the Rouge Assembly Plant, where he worked until he retired. With the extra money, we rented an upper-floor flat on Tuxedo near Dexter Boulevard. Six days a week, I took the bus from Dexter to West Grand Boulevard to Woodward Avenue, downtown to the building where I worked, directly behind Hudson's. This trip was not easy for me because riding a bus or being in other confined spaces such as elevators made me feel like I couldn't breathe, like I couldn't get out. (Eventually I overcame this fear, which resulted from my experience in the hayloft and impacted me for years in ways I couldn't have predicted.) My father worked the night shift at Ford, and on his wages we could pay the rent; my income paid for our food. Little by little, we accumulated enough money to rent a small upper apartment in a single house owned by an old lady who lived on the main floor with her daughter. I lived there until I was married.

Women continued to be interested in my father, and he was interested in them. I begged him to get remarried, as much for his sake as my own. I felt responsible for my father, and he needed someone to take care of him. At the same time, I longed to have my own life. It was a good time in my life. Boys were plentiful. I was always the smiling one; I danced and sang and was pleasant to be around. No one ever knew what I had been through.

Married Life

Imet Herb in 1956 at a B'nai B'rith dance. I was there with a group of young male friends, but I was not going steady with any of them. Herb was there with a date, but somehow he managed to get my telephone number. I refused to talk with him until one day, several weeks later, when I saw him at Sandy Beach, several miles north of Detroit. There he was, flexing his muscles. He just wouldn't give up on me. He was so sweet and caring; it's easy to fall in love with those qualities. To this day, I feel as though I'm lucky.

Herb and me in 1969.

Herb had a brother who was ten years older, as well as a half-brother and a half-sister from his father's previous marriage. Herb's half-brother owned Gorman's Furniture, a successful Detroit-area business.

I always say "we got engaged in bed" to see the reaction this gets from people! I was laid up with a bad cold, and Herb brought me some chicken soup to cheer me up and make me feel better. He knelt by the bed and proposed! He didn't have any money to buy me an engagement ring, so he gave me his bar mitzvah ring, and that became my engagement ring. Those things don't matter when you're in love!

At this time in my life, I was focused on not talking about the past so that I could lead a "normal" life. I wanted to become very American, as I said before. This is partly why I married a Detroit-born American man and not a fellow survivor. I knew of many survivors who married other survivors, but I wanted to build a life with someone from outside the circle. Maybe if I had married a survivor, I would have explored my past sooner than I did.

My father gave me a $1,000 to pay for a wedding, and Herb made up the rest because I didn't earn very much with my work. We had a beautiful wedding, so fun and gay, on October 19th, 1957, and we started a life together. We had many responsibilities between his family and my father. Everybody liked me because I always had a smile and a hug for everyone. Herb had five or six uncles and aunts, and we became the center of it all. I was craving this; I wanted a family. My first birthday celebration ever was while we were engaged, and Herb's mother baked me a cake. His mother was so sweet. I used to like to hug her the way I hugged my grandfather. She was "mushy" like he was, and it reminded me of him. I was so fortunate to be taken in by the entire family. My father was also included. He lived with us in a flat on Tyler and Dexter until he could afford to buy a small duplex in Detroit.

Herb worked as an engineer, running a design room with many draftsmen under him at Koltanbar Engineering, where they designed automotive assembly tooling. His firm was a subcontractor for Ford Motor Company. Herb made a good wage, and we felt fortunate. He was a very ambitious young man and wanted to make it on his own, but he knew that to compete in engineering, he needed connections that he didn't have. Being Jewish in those days didn't help. He was always taken with the possibilities and potential of having his own business, so he was very interested when a friend suggested that he try the vending machine business. Herb and a friend bought a cigarette machine and placed it in an apartment house. We refilled it at night. It's funny, I never felt so wealthy as I did that first time I collected the coins, spread them out on the kitchen table, and counted all of them! Cigarettes sold for twenty-five cents a pack. Sales were fair, but I never felt so rich! Unfortunately, people would break into the machine and steal the contents, so it ended up costing us money! Still, Herb and his friend started placing more cigarette machines around the area, and eventually another friend approached them to form a three-way partnership. The business expanded, but Herb kept working as an engineer until the business could support all three families. Our garage was both the office and the place where we kept the merchandise. The other two partners would come over at 5:00 a.m. to get supplies; the neighbors must have thought we were running a brothel!

Our son Mark was born on September 17, 1959, followed by Robert (Bobby) on August 28, 1962. The children were such a joy to me. I wanted a large family, but I had several miscarriages and couldn't have any more children, so I feel blessed to have the two. I believe large families are wonderful, maybe because I didn't have one myself.

During these years, I only wanted to look at happiness in the face. I wanted to see and try everything and experience everything. I constantly showed a pleasant demeanor and a smiling face. I was always ready to do anything fun, even things that were somewhat daring.

There were hard times as well, however. When Herb was thirty-four years old and the boys were eight and five, he had an impacted wisdom tooth extracted. A swelling formed in the aftermath and kept getting larger. The doctor was baffled by this, and after several consultations, a biopsy was taken. Herb had developed osteosarcoma of the right mandible, or a cancerous tumor on his jaw. His doctor referred us to a specialist in head and neck surgery in New York. The specialist had a very stern demeanor and an abrupt manner of speaking, and he didn't give us much hope during the first examination. We decided to have him perform surgery to remove the tumor, so we rushed home, arranged for my mother-in-law to take care of our sons, and hurried back to New York. The surgeon removed half of Herb's lower jaw and part of his tongue. The surgery was long and extensive, and the doctor didn't give us any hope.

When I saw Herb following the surgery, he was in terrible shape. He was covered with tubes. He had a tracheotomy and couldn't talk. Everyone could understand his gestures without him even speaking. A nurse sat by the bed for the first few days to suction his trachea, and then I took over. The doctor tried to reconstruct Herb's jaw with a graft from his hip bone, and he said we would just have to wait and see what would happen. We didn't know if Herb was going to live or die. Fortunately, we had wonderful friends, some who traveled from Detroit to New York at various times to give us support.

After three weeks in New York, Herb was still hospitalized; his body rejected the bone graft. I came home for a few days to see the children, and when I went back to the hospital, I continued to help with Herb's nursing care. The wound was allowed to granulate, so instead of sewing it up, the doctor let it heal layer by layer. I helped suction Herb whenever necessary. I wasn't horrified; I just became numb, like I always had under stress. I just did what needed to be done. It took a year for Herb to recover. For the next five years, a local doctor performed follow-up care, and we made trips twice a year to New York to see the doctor there. Thank God the sarcoma never recurred.

After Herb returned home to continue his recovery, he fell into a deep depression, and I took care to make sure it didn't get worse. I forced him to take a walk every day and to enjoy his time with the children, who became used to seeing him look very different than he had before. Herb's jaw didn't align correctly when it healed because he didn't have all his teeth. Before the surgery, he had been handsome, with a cleft chin and dimples like Kirk Douglas; now that part of his face was missing, he was petrified that everyone would turn away from him. He eventually grew a beard, and that helped him gain confidence. Still, his personality changed. When we first met and married, he was extremely ambitious in his engineering career. After the surgery, he had a different outlook on life, and our priorities changed. Herb became less ambitious, and his work became less important. Doing things for others and being with his family were his main focus. As a result, we always "looked at the flowers," in appreciation for the good things that came our way.

Getting Help

I first became aware of the intensity of my nightmares after I was married. Prior to that, there was no one to tell me that I was moaning and crying in my sleep. Although I was having nightmares, I didn't know why and didn't let myself think about it. I always awoke with a sense of heaviness and, if I'd had a nightmare, a feeling of fear. I'd never slept well, and I was usually exhausted when I awoke, a sign that my sleep was being disturbed. I dreamed about being buried or about being killed, although the nightmare always stopped right before the point of death. Sometimes there was something like a large sphere looming over me in my dreams. When Herb woke me up, I would always say, "I'm afraid." He would take me in his arms, comfort me, and the nightmare would be gone for that night.

Although my immediate and extended family knew that I was a survivor, they didn't know any of the details. My son Mark was the first one to begin asking me about my experiences. In school, he was assigned to write about the background of his parents, but when he asked me about my family, I replied, "Someday I'll think about it and tell you." When I did discuss my youth, I only offered him minimal information, mostly talking about Metz after the war. He never asked my father for any details, but he frequently asked me. His questions were among my first motivations to begin dealing with my memories.

Herb also didn't know my story, other than the basic fact that I had survived in an attic or hayloft. I never told him. Who wanted to talk about it? I don't want to talk about it now! And as I've already said, I was always the smiling one. Always. Nobody ever knew me to be otherwise. So I'm sure it was a shock to my family and friends when my past overwhelmed me and I could no longer function.

I've already described how seeing the skinhead on television in the early 1980s, when I was in my late forties, brought back the horror of the Holocaust to me, and I lost control of my bladder. After this experience, I became upset; as I continued to dwell on why my body had reacted as it did, I felt ashamed. It felt like I had the stench with me all the time. I remember thinking, why was I so upset with this program? In time, I fell deeper and deeper into depression, unable to deal with all the feelings and fears. I didn't even want to get up in the morning. After several months, I concluded that I needed to get help from a doctor. I made this decision because of my family; I knew I was hurting them. I could see it on their faces. I have always been very stubborn in the belief that I could resolve everything myself, that I didn't need help, that I could accomplish anything on my own. Given the intensity of the thoughts and feelings that start flooding in on top of the depression, however, I recognized that I could not conquer my problems alone.

My previous experiences with psychiatrists had not been good. When I first came to the United States, before I was married, I went to Sinai Hospital in Detroit for medical treatment because the hospital was offering free care and we didn't have any medical insurance. One psychiatrist asked me if I had any sexual fantasies. I gave some sort of answer and never went back. To me, this was an improper question. Another time, my father was applying for compensation from the German government, and the process required that I be interviewed by a psychiatrist who would decide whether or not my problems were real and if my claim was legitimate. In one session! The first thing the psychiatrist asked me was about my sex life! How often did I have sex? I told him several times a day and never went back to him either. In those days, it was unheard of for even doctors to ask questions like that. To me, unless someone is having sexual problems, this is a superficial question. I don't understand trying to relate sex to a very painful, non-sexual experience such as the Holocaust. My father became angry that I wouldn't talk to the psychiatrist, so I wrote a letter to the psychiatrist saying I was really terrified and didn't remember anything, that I freeze when I'm asked if I remember the past. My father was approved for a minimal amount of compensation, and so was I; Suzanne totally refused the money. Ultimately, I decided the money should go into a special charitable fund. I couldn't take anything from the Germans. Perhaps if I had really needed the money, I might have taken it, but I didn't and I don't.

After I had decided to seek help, my primary physician recommended a doctor who was chief of psychiatry at Sinai Hospital. At my first session, I asked him, "Are you going to ask me about my sex life? I don't want that." He replied, "No, let's talk about anything. What do you want to tell me?" "What do you want me to say? What do you want to know?" I responded. He answered, "Talk about anything." I didn't want to talk about just anything, however; I wanted him to ask me specific questions! We went on this way for a couple of sessions. I didn't know where to start, and he didn't ask specific questions for the first month or so. In fact, he rarely spoke to me in those early sessions; it was up to me to do the talking.

In the beginning, my need for help was so great that we met two or three days a week. Sometimes I went to his office only to sit for an hour and not say a word. Months passed before I could start talking at length, yet sometimes I would freeze and couldn't talk at all. I remember him telling me that this would pass, it would get better. He was, and still is, a very nice man. When you're not familiar with the process, you don't know how to start. I did appreciate that even though he's in the Freudian way of thinking, he didn't push me in the area of questioning my sex life. The only thing I ever told him along those lines was that I never saw my parents embrace or hug.

Someday I'd like to have the transcripts from my early sessions. My doctor has promised that he will give them to me when he retires, but he thinks it will be very difficult on me to review them. I told my doctor, "Okay, you hold my hand." I always have to turn things into a joke.

One day, the doctor asked me to come to his house for a session on the weekend; I later found out that he often worked with very ill patients in his home on Saturdays. When I got there, I sat in my car in front of his house for twenty or thirty minutes, unable to face being questioned again. When I finally walked in and sat down, he asked me which concentration camp I had been in. He *angered* me with this question! I always felt the concentration-camp people were the only ones who seemed to matter to others in terms of being a true survivor. I felt "hidden children" like me were made to feel that our suffering was not as intense or as worthy of attention and sympathy. I was upset that I didn't have a number on my arm as visible proof of my pain and suffering. I was angry at him. Very angry. And I told him so. I said, "I don't want to be angry at you, it's not me. I want to be friends with you, but I don't think I can. I don't know what to say to you." I told him I was never in a concentration camp. Prior to this meeting I had told him some things about my parents, very benign, everyday details, but this time when he asked me directly about my parents, I again became angry. I wanted to leave his study. He directed his questions to how my mother died, and that's when a breakthrough finally happened for me. Words and emotions began pouring out of me. Some new memory or thought jumped into my brain every minute. I was feeling the past so strongly that it was as if I were living it at that very moment. The therapy process had finally begun.

At the same time, my depression remained destructive. I couldn't get out of bed; I was afraid to face my husband, and I was afraid to face the day and my psychiatrist. My doctor had me try several medications, but they always made me ill. I knew the medications would take several weeks before they had any effect, but I needed to end the pain immediately, not in several weeks! It took a while until we found the right combination that helped me. My heart was hurting, and my chest was exploding. I hardly knew what was going on around me. I would pass people by without acknowledging them. I felt uncomfortable, as though others were looking at me in a strange way, knowing I was ill. I tried to hide. I wore a red hat with a large brim so no one would see me. I was in a different world of emotions, like when I was in the hayloft. I tried to grasp onto what I once was, but it wasn't there; I was in a dark gulf.

In the beginning, Herb often asked me about the doctor and his methods, but I was unable to tell him one word of what I was talking about in my sessions; they were much too vivid to describe to him. It came to a point where I didn't want to live; I was actually becoming suicidal. The depression overcame me, and I didn't see any other way out. Everyone around me knew I was very ill. I totally withdrew, dwelling on the terrible thoughts that were filling my brain. Most of the time, however, I managed to stay functioning, doing what I had to do. Depression is such a horrible disease; I can understand why people with depression are so desperate that they see no way out except to die. Some may wonder, how could they do it? Well, I know—it's such a deep gulf that suicide seems the only way out. I indeed wanted to die, but I thought about the pain my action would bring upon my children and husband.

Years ago, when our children were in high school, our next-door neighbors had a daughter who suffered from depression. She had tried to commit suicide several times, but her mother would always find her in time. One day, the mother came rushing over to our house, hysterical because she couldn't get into her house. I went with her, and we discovered that her daughter had killed herself by running the car in the closed garage. She had written a small note and left it on the door going into the kitchen, saying "Mother, father, I cannot do it any more." I took the mother outside and called 911. The girl had been smart enough to act "normal," so her parents thought she was getting better, but she was just waiting for another opportunity. That was another tragedy in my life.

I never told my psychiatrist that I was suicidal. During our sessions, I would get angry at him and scream, "Do you know how much pain I feel inside? Do you know how much pain you bring by asking questions?" He'd say, "Erna, I know." And that would make me feel a little better, maybe until the next session. The pain was so crushing, it was as though my chest was going to explode. Months later I asked him if he knew there were times I didn't want to live. He said, "I knew." I asked, "Do you enjoy seeing people cry all the time?" Some people fall in love with therapy and their therapists, but I began to hate him.

Eventually, I went to therapy only three times a week, then once a week, and then once a month. After about two years of frequent sessions with my doctor, the transition to the final phase of having therapy only once a month was a time of extreme terror and fear for my entire family and for me. I never told Herb one word about what was happening, and he was kind enough to understand that I just couldn't. In the second year of my therapy, he bought me a tape recorder and suggested I start recording whatever was on my mind, whatever was flowing in me, even if it was just crying. I spent months and months speaking whatever came into my mind. I only recorded my thoughts when I was by myself. This was at the height of my depression. I was suicidal at times because I couldn't bear the pain. I remember screaming into the tape recorder. There was no sequence to my memories or events. Everything was just pell-mell, mixed up. I just released whatever came into my mind. My memories didn't make sense, but I kept searching them because I desperately *needed* them to make sense. Of course, that didn't happen. I hid the tapes in a new place every day so no one could listen, not even Herb, although I knew he would never do so without permission. They were so full of pain. I just didn't want anyone else to hear them.

Finally, two or three years after I began taping my thoughts, I reviewed some of the tapes and began to realize a sequence of events, and that was when I made my first tape that had some logic to it. I tried to talk to my sister about my memories in an effort to determine if they were correct, but she refused to listen to me. At that time, I didn't know if what I was remembering was real or just a product of my imagination. At one point, I let Herb and my two sons, who were home from college for our High Holidays, Rosh Hashana and Yom Kippur, hear the tape I had made of my memories so they could better understand what had happened to me. I seated them in front of the tape player and turned it on. However, I could not bear to see the hurt on their faces as they listened to what I had endured, so I left the house. When I returned, I saw three grown men holding each other and crying. Herb didn't know any of the things I started to discover while under psychiatric care. These were things that even I hadn't known before. Until then, I only wanted to laugh and smile. I'm two personalities, probably.

It took a long time, many years, before I began to feel better. When I did my first interview with Dr. Sidney Bolkosky, a professor and Holocaust researcher at the

University of Michigan-Dearborn, in 1984, I was not
through the depression yet. I had good days and bad days.
Not that I had anything more to say, but I still had the
emotions. I never felt that I had control of my life. I always had to take care of other people. I never lived on my
own and have never been without responsibility for others.

I have been in therapy for over twenty years now. I've
been going for so long that I sometimes ask the doctor
what kind of car he drives as a result of my visits! Although
I continue to need the medications, I think I really
stopped needing therapy itself when I was in my late six-
ties. I have worked out my own techniques for dealing
with problems. When I am feeling especially down, I can
say to myself, I have this feeling or that feeling, but I know
it will pass, and I'm going to sit and wait until it passes.
That's the technique I use. My feeling of depression is
probably cyclical, although I don't think it's seasonal. I
don't see gray days as gray days; they are just another day.
In saying that whatever is bothering me will pass, I am ultimately saying, I don't need someone else to solve this.
There's no use in telling my doctor about my troubles because they will pass! He and I mostly just talk about what
is currently going on in my life; we are like two friends
catching up with each other. He says I'm one of a kind.
The intense therapy I underwent with him many years
ago was an extremely painful experience. Although there
were times when I hated him, he's just wonderful to me
now; he tells me all the time how great I am. He tells me
I have a low opinion of myself, that I feel that whatever I
do, it's not enough. Indeed, I'm very hard on myself and

always think I could have done more. He boosts me with the perspective that, although I've lived a difficult life, I have done incredibly well, especially in my work with Holocaust education. He keeps encouraging me, which means a lot coming from him. I don't truly believe it myself, and the feeling of inadequacy is something that will probably never go away. He has said to me many times, "Erna, you're a very accomplished person. You're a fabulous person and you just don't realize it." And I don't. Ultimately, my years of therapy were a time of great pain, but I made it through and finally came to terms with myself.

Undoubtedly, whatever stability I have now is due not only to my work with my psychiatrist, but to my husband, Herb. He is wonderful! Herb is totally devoted to me and always supportive, and I am very fortunate. He is another one of my miracles. My sister didn't get that kind of help from her husband, and maybe that's why she turned into the person she became. She couldn't shake the "victimness" of her life.

It all comes down to this: I hope my mother is proud of me for the kind of human being I am. I must have been influenced by her or inherited genes and qualities from her because I am totally different from my sister, who took after my father. I have always had success with the way people see me on the outside, although what this success means, I don't know. People will tell you that I always had a smile; I was outgoing and striving to make friends. Nobody really knew *me*, however; they just saw the smile

127

that I put on for everybody. On the inside, I strove to purge myself of the bitterness. I don't know if I accomplished this, but I think I did. A person can't live with bitterness and come out whole, and I think I did come out whole. I have the ability to forgive. I think all of this comes from my mother; she must have been like that.

I truly wish I could have known my mother. It's hard not having a real mental image of my mother, of a real human being who loves and hates. Was she a yeller? Was she huggable? Was she strict? If I had that image, I could understand her better, and perhaps understand myself better, too. I can still feel her body shaking when we were in peril, and I remember her smell during her period; I remember her having little pieces of cloth to use for sanitary pads. I remember her wearing only skirts. I only have these very small, random memories of her. I feel sorry that I didn't have the privilege of truly knowing her, good or bad. Everything was just abruptly cut off, leaving me with many unanswered questions and unresolved issues.

When I refer to my father, I call him Papa, which is a fond term of endearment, but I don't use the similarly endearing Mama when I refer to my mother. I discussed this with my therapist, and he suggested that this is the result of my anger. I remember being angry with her when she died, but I don't have any other recollections of being angry with her. I have a soft feeling and an angry feeling about my father, but there's no softness for my mother. How terrible is it for a child not to cry when her mother dies, or to stand around a cot when her mother is covered with lice and vermin and not cry? To be dead inside and not have any feelings? Yet I *am* a soft, caring person; my father wasn't like that, so I must have gotten it from my mother. My mother has given me this gift of being soft, which is a gift of understanding, feeling, and always trying to help. I'm grateful to my mother because I think I have her demeanor.

When I speak to children, I always tell them, "You all have mothers because you're here; you were born. You know whether your mother is good, or if she screams at you, or if she bosses you. You know some mothers are pleasant or harsh, squishy or cold, but I never had that opportunity to know any of those things about my mother, good or bad, and I think you should cherish whatever types of people your parents or grandparents are, because you'll value them later in life when you understand their motives better." I want them to treasure what they have in their lives. I want them to appreciate their family a little more.

My years of therapy were a time of great pain, but I made it through and finally came to terms with myself.

The Hidden Children Group

In 1992, the Hidden Children Conference, an event to bring together those of us who were forced as youngsters to go into hiding to escape Nazi persecution, was held in Washington, D.C. The Anti-Defamation League (ADL) was the main sponsor for the conference. I was encouraged by Dr. Sidney Bolkosky to attend. He knew other child survivors from the Detroit area who were going, so I decided to go as well. Conference planners expected 500 attendees, and 1500 showed up! I didn't realize there were so many other child survivors; it was overwhelming but very exciting at the same time.

Left: Participants of the Hidden Children's conference at the United States Holocaust Memorial Museum in the mid-2000s. Upper right: Members of our Detroit-area Hidden Children group in 2006.

Most of the attendees had never spoken about their experiences to others; just like me, they had never revealed their pasts. Each story that I listened to was similar yet quite different from one another.

While I was at the conference, I met a young woman who lived in Washington, D.C. She was younger than most of the others in attendance, and she was weeping that she had been born at the end of the war but didn't know to whom. She was hoping to find something about her past at the conference. It struck me that she was crying and upset because she had no idea where she came from. She was looking for some string or connection, something to hold. That was a very profound experience for me. When we came home, I went to every workshop and meeting about the Holocaust. I still spoke Russian and understood Polish at the time. I sat and listened but don't recall any of the stories I heard.

I made several contacts and connections at the conference, and a few of us, including Helen Bennett, Rene Lichtman, Ina Silbergleit, Stefa Kupfer, and Giselle Feldman, decided to form our own survivors group in the Detroit area. We placed notices at all the local synagogues and in the *Jewish News* to announce that we were forming a group of hidden children and encouraging others like us to join. Little by little, people began calling us. I think every synagogue in Michigan put our notice on their bulletin boards or in their newsletters. The Anti-Defamation League was very kind at the beginning. They allowed us to use space for meetings until we decided to meet in our homes because it was more intimate. We agreed that no spouses could attend unless they were also hidden children. No camp survivors, either; just hidden children.

Some people feel as though hidden children are not really Holocaust survivors. After I once spoke at the Holocaust Memorial Center in metropolitan Detroit, I stopped in the center's gift shop to look through some books. A woman who knew I was a speaker approached me and said, "You're not a Holocaust survivor." I said, "Ma'am, please don't say that. I've heard that so many times. We are the only ones left. If you think I'm not a Holocaust survivor, I tell you I buried my own mother." I was so taken aback by what she said to me. It was always as if the hidden children didn't count. Hidden children constantly encountered this bias, thus the need for our group.

The group was very important to all of us. People came to meetings to spill out their stories and emotions. The group usually met in my home. It was like a kinship, a real family. When we saw each other, we were happy. There were no hassles or conflicts to speak of. We gravitated to each other initially because of our like experiences and to share our individual stories. Some members didn't want to go beyond the original concept of the meetings as therapeutic sessions, but in time others wanted to broaden our purpose. Thus the Holocaust Education Coalition was formed, with Betty Elias as president. An educator and daughter of survivors, Betty had assisted Dr. Bolkosky in developing a school curriculum titled *Life Un-*

worthy of Life for teachers to use in their classrooms when presenting units about the Holocaust. Several of us decided we wanted to support the effort to distribute the curriculum to schools. For several years the coalition held fundraisers so that we could provide the materials to schools at no cost.

Rev. Jim Lyons, a local minister from the Ecumenical Institute who was active in Holocaust education, was an integral part of the coalition. He was an inspiring personality who taught school and church groups about the Holocaust. His presentations included interactive experiences that were meant to make participants truly feel the emotions that a hidden child might have felt.

The coalition's efforts are still ongoing, but I am no longer involved. However, I am still active in the Hidden Children group, and we meet monthly. I go to the annual Hidden Children conferences, which are held around the world, and I even helped organize the 2006 conference that was held in Dearborn, Michigan.

Why I Speak about My Experiences

I began feeling uneasy about not being involved with the idea of Holocaust remembrance when the first Holocaust museum in the Detroit area, the Holocaust Memorial Center, was built in West Bloomfield in the early 1980s. I knew the rabbi in charge of the center because for years he had belonged to the same synagogue as my father. Little by little, the rabbi drew me in to become more involved. Herb and I also donated a plaque in my parents' names.

Upper left: Me speaking about my experiences.
Right: One of many letters I've received from people who have attended my presentations.

Over the course of a number of years beginning in the late 1970s, a series of Holocaust-related movies and events impacted my life. In 1978, the miniseries *Holocaust* was broadcast on network television. Although it was highly acclaimed, I decided not to watch it, which added to my guilt, although I really didn't understand why I felt guilty. In 1984, I began my series of interviews with Dr. Sidney Bolkosky, a professor and Holocaust researcher. Then the movie *Shoah*, directed by Claude Lanzmann, came out in 1985 and was shown over two nights at the Detroit Film Theatre. The movie was about the Holocaust, particularly the trains, the camps, and Auschwitz. Lanzmann located several survivors in Israel and interviewed them for the film. I was most impacted by the story of a barber at Auschwitz who was ordered to shave the heads of new arrivals before they were put into the gas chambers. At times he encountered people he knew. As he was relating his story in the movie, he was crying and reliving everything, even though he was now safe. The movie followed the man to his hometown in Poland, where people were interviewed in front of the local church. Lanzmann wanted to see if people's opinions about Jews had changed since the war. They hadn't. They still hated Jews. The people were surprised to see the man was still alive. They laughed and made anti-Semitic slurs, wondering how any Jews had survived. There was a lot of hatred. My experience seeing that movie was crushing to me. I was particularly affected by the movie's inclusion of a clay scale model of the *schlauch*, a tunnel or tube through which prisoners arriving at Auschwitz were rushed to get to an undressing area before they went into the showers and gas chambers. That image stayed with me; I had the feeling that I should have been in there, and this added to my guilt feelings. I always see this clip from that film in front of my eyes. For many years I would ask myself, how come I wasn't in there? Guilt over my survival constantly plagued me during those years, but now I am just amazed that I survived.

As I mentioned, I was making my audio tapes, but I wouldn't even allow Herb to listen to them. My memories and emotions were just coming out in bunches and I was very ill. A friend of mine urged me to meet Dr. Bolkosky. She knew that he was doing interviews with Holocaust survivors and that he had a reputation for being very sympathetic and a knowledgeable historian. My friend was in a group that supported young musicians, and she invited me to go to a concert with her, at which I finally met the professor.

I was still dealing with my raw emotions, but one day I decided to call Dr. Bolkosky. He asked if I wanted to do an interview right away, but I replied, "No, just listen to one of my tapes," which he did. Later, we did a long interview, and I remember it clearly. I was relieved when the interview was over, and I was glad that he was going to create a permanent record of my story. He was deeply moved. When I was walking out after the interview, I was laughing. When I get upset, quite often I laugh instead of verbally expressing my emotions, thus my unusual behavior. This interview was how I got started telling my story. He met with me several times; the interviews are preserved in the Voice/Vision Holocaust Survivor Oral History Archive at the University of Michigan-Dearborn (http://holocaust.umd.umich.edu).

Soon, other survivors started urging me to speak to groups at the Holocaust Memorial Center. At the time, I didn't know how to do this, and emotionally I wasn't ready. Someone I knew said, "Come listen to me," so I went. Someone else asked if I would go speak to a small class, and I agreed. That's how I started speaking to groups. Recently, I spoke to a group of high-school students, and a boy approached me afterward and said that it had been his grandmother who was the person who had first urged me to tell my story in public. I had accompanied her to the Holocaust Memorial Center, where she spoke about her experiences. She introduced me and asked me to come up. I had never spoken to strangers about what I had been through; to me it was very private, but suddenly there I was, starting to open myself up. I was ill at ease and quite emotional, so she held my hand while I spoke.

Soon afterwards, Rev. Jim Lyons also invited me to talk about my experiences in a video interview that was shown on local cable television. I had spoken a couple of times at the Holocaust Memorial Center, and he may have heard me there. He was teaching children in the Sunday schools about the Holocaust, and he wanted them to understand what it was like for a Holocaust child.

During this time, public interest in the events and details of the Holocaust was on the rise, and my story stood out somewhat because I was a hidden child, not a camp survivor. I spoke to small groups as well as on some radio programs. I also did interviews with psychologists working with traumatized children; about a dozen academic papers were written about me. Word spread that I would talk. Schools and colleges such as Lawrence Technological University and Bowling Green University invited me to speak several times. During several summers, I spoke at a week-long seminar for high-school graduates who were considered Michigan's brightest future leaders.

The people who come to listen to me speak about prejudice and the effects of violence understand what I am saying. I am also on the lookout for the deniers. Some children are not exposed to learning about what's right and wrong; hate and prejudice have been so ingrained into their make-up that they're unable to separate from it. Those are the ones I am targeting when I speak. I remember being invited to speak to a local business group that was "men-only." Two hundred men attended the luncheon, and I don't think there was one Jewish person in the group. After I spoke, many came up and said, "You know, we needed to hear this and to be told." They appreciated my message about trying to be less prejudicial. One of them sent me a moving letter about his Korean War experience. He wrote at great length about a mass murder that his unit had been involved with; I think he was clearing his soul a little bit. I still have the letter.

As the years in which I was actively telling my story went by, I started to examine myself from a new perspective. Why don't I hate people? Why don't I blame anybody for what happened to me? Why don't I hate the Poles or Ukrainians or Germans? I realized that I had a larger message to convey to people beyond my little story. Some people noted that my story was a little similar to Anne Frank's, and for a while I was sort of known as the French Anne Frank. This led me to ask myself, why am I alive and why isn't Anne Frank? So I began speaking about what hatred and prejudice can do to an individual. As I went along, I received many letters, first from teachers and then from students. Little by little, I discovered that my story is only important in making people understand the extent to which we continuously perpetuate hatred. Too many parents teach hatred in the home by using slurs or discriminatory comments every day. People become accustomed to labeling others and deciding whether to hate them or not based upon those labels. Exposing the effect of this hatred became my focus over the years.

Children aren't born with hate. They have to learn it. A line from the song "You've Got to Be Carefully Taught" from the musical *South Pacific* states this idea very well: "You've got to be taught before it's too late,/Before you are six or seven or eight,/To hate all the people your relatives hate–/You've got to be carefully taught!"

Indeed, I discovered I was serving a larger purpose in sharing my story. At the end of my talk, I speak about what's going on in the world today and our responsibility as human beings. It's almost like preaching, but it isn't; it comes from the bottom of my heart. This is the part I feel good about. I tell audiences and individuals that I don't want their sympathy, but instead I want them to see my story as an example of what can happen and is happening in other parts of the world. My story has ties to the experiences of the Armenians decades ago and those of some tribes in Africa today: this is what happens when nobody stands up to stop the slaughter. As humans, we have an obligation not to tolerate these horrors. To be a bystander is almost as bad as being a perpetrator. We have to consciously choose the way we do things and treat others, especially in the United States, where we seem to be more involved in acquiring material things. When we see a hungry child, we don't reach out. When we see war footage on television, it seems like it's far away. Real life is not like a John Wayne movie, in which a character stands up and walks away from the set after being shot. When we see the starving children in the world, victims of malnutrition or hunger, that's real. It's not the same as missing one meal. It destroys them. I remember those days, of being hungry, with nothing to eat from hour to hour.

I'm grateful that maybe I changed a few lives for the better. Maybe my story helped someone who has similar pain or was unhappy in his or her childhood cope with life. After I speak, it's not unusual for rape victims to approach me to share their stories; they are desperate to understand how I could deal with such emotional stress in my life. I specifically remember one woman who had been laughing happily with her family just moments before she took me aside and said, "I have traumas in my life. How are you able not to hate?" I replied, "You have to decide to let this go and look to the future. You have to decide that; no one can do it for you. *You* have to let it go."

I think I've made a difference in many children's lives, if only to make them feel that if they don't get love from family members, if they don't get the attention they need, or if they're being abused in one form or another, they can overcome it. I want them to recognize that they are the parents of the future. I tell them about my lack of formal schooling in order to demonstrate that, nevertheless, I pushed ahead. When I look at myself clearly, I know I have nothing to be ashamed of. I've done the right things.

Another message I promote is related to the dangerous concepts of entitlement and instant gratification, which is especially prominent among some young people. They think that adults, the world, the community owes them and should make their lives easy. They want everything right now. I want them to know that if they work and actively pursue what they want instead of expecting it to be handed to them, they will overcome obstacles. I have addressed prison inmates in their teens and early twenties. I try to make them understand that one reason they are where they are is because they thought they could get things easily. Once after I spoke and told my story to a group of inmates, I asked them what they wanted to do with their lives after they were freed. Each one started telling me their hopes and plans. I asked them what they were good at. Some said they were good with woodworking. I said, "Why are you here? Why not strive to do what comes easily to you?" One young man said he wanted to go to law school and become like Johnny Cochran. I said, "Law sounds terrific, but what's wrong with being yourself and a lawyer as well and helping the poor?" I have letters and beautiful drawings from them. It was a moving experience. One person that stands out in my mind was a guy who stood up and said, "I grew up in a home where bigotry was part of a daily life. How can I change that?" I told him, "You just stood up and told me your home was bigoted. Just doing this is a beginning. It means you really want that to change."

I've been interviewed by many psychologists and psychiatrists, some while they were working on their degrees. One in particular irritated me to no end. He said, "I could interview you over the phone." I said, "What? Interview me over the phone?" He could sense I was angry, and he said he'd come to my home if I was still willing. He came over to talk, but during the interview he spoke lightly, as if he were entertaining me. When we were finished and he was walking out, he asked me, "Why are all Holocaust survivors rich?" I angrily replied, "You are asking me to give you painful memories, and you are taking this like it's some sort of soap opera." The survivors he knew only happened to be well off. They worked like the devil and made sacrifices to achieve whatever financial security they had. No one gave it to them; they didn't steal it. I don't know why he had that opinion, but I made it clear to him that he was wrong.

People who care for abused children or who are studying child psychology often seek me out, but I have nothing to tell them because I'm not affected the way they think I might be or in the way that would support their work. I am in full control of my choices, and I choose the path of looking at the flowers rather than dwelling on hatred. In every one of my speeches, I talk about the choices that farmer made long ago. He had options—he didn't have to help my family, but he chose to do so, and he saved our lives. We all have choices. One person made a choice, and that's why I'm here. It's very important. Every human being has a choice.

I have a stack of many fabulous letters from those who have heard me speak, and in fact, I've had several students correspond with me regularly over many years. Occasionally, they call me. It shows that somehow I connected with them. They have depth of understanding and feeling. That's what I'm trying to touch in people when I give my talk. Maybe it's presumptuous of me to think I can do that, but at least I'm trying. We live in a very cruel world right now; I feel sorry for the young people. I wish somehow we could turn things around, but I really don't see that happening. If my talk helps someone defend the little boy or girl in the school courtyard that is being mocked, or if it makes someone extend a hand or give a word of kindness, it is worthwhile. My first-grade experience is very vivid in my mind, and I constantly channel my thoughts through that context. If someone had just said hi to me or physically touched me in a compassionate way, it might have made a huge difference.

Children can be so cruel, and they don't know the damage they can inflict. They don't understand the results or the harm that they do.

There comes a time when people have to assess themselves and take responsibility for their own lives. In my talks, I also usually mention that my father was a heavy drinker. I'd rather not have to admit this, but there are many children who live with alcoholics, and I want them to recognize that, if they can look a little bit beyond their situation and try to not let it affect them too badly, they can lead a happy, healthy life. I share that I overcame the impact of my father's drinking, even though it caused me to have to go to work so I could put food on our family's table instead of going to school . I hope to inspire other children of alcoholics to see that they too can overcome their situation. Not all parents can take care of their children; instead, the child might need to take care of the parent.

Do I get satisfaction out of speaking? No, but it helps me when I talk about my mother and about how terrible I feel that I didn't even cry when we buried her. It's sort of like asking forgiveness of her. My talks also give me the feeling that I am somewhat repaying that farmer for giving me life by publicly acknowledging him, even though I don't know his name. I owe a debt to my father and my mother because they went through hell to keep us alive. I also feel that I owe a debt to those who did not survive the Holocaust. They have no voice. I realize that I am nearing the end of my life. If I don't speak now, I will soon

145

find myself out of time to do so; in fact, pretty soon there will be no one left to speak. Ultimately, I am privileged to be here. I appreciate life so much. Why was it given to me? Why, indeed? This is a question that I ask myself over and over again. I have such a wonderful life! It's true. I met a great guy, and he has given me love and comfort. I appreciated the gift of my life even more in the last twenty years, since I started to recall and deal with all my memories. Maybe as humans we have to suffer a little to appreciate life.

I do see a downside to the attention paid to the victims and survivors of the Holocaust. With the mass media promoting a range of real and fictionalized stories, and with the many museums and memorials that sprung up following the opening of Yad Vashem in Israel in the 1950s, the Holocaust became an industry. The over-commercialization of that era worries me. Many speakers I know charge a fee for their appearances, but I could never accept anything for speaking. If payment is offered, I give it back to the school or group. How could I use that money? If I needed the money to eat, maybe it would be different, but to buy myself something frivolous because of my past experience—no way, no way! Teachers at C. L. Phelps Middle School in Ishpeming, Michigan, once offered me a check for $200 for speaking there, but I refused to take it. I knew the teachers were working on a small grant, and I told them to put it back into their budget. It is not important to me to be compensated for telling my story.

Unlike me, my father never told his story to anyone that I know of, certainly not in my presence nor to me or my sister. We never talked about it. Never. Maybe it was my fault because I never broached the subject. I wanted to be like everyone else when I came to the United States: I wanted to become an American. I realize now that I should have spoken with my father about what happened to us. Why didn't I? Probably because I had other distractions and obligations. I was busy with my own responsibilities, with building my life with Herb and helping others. We didn't have the time or the interest to get into it. When Herb and I married, I became very close to my mother-in-law. We were more than just mother-in-law and daughter-in-law. She would tell me all her stories; I became her confidante. Why didn't I do this with my father? Yet even my mother-in-law never knew my story. I have gone from being unable to discuss my experiences with the people I loved most to being willing to share them with strangers because of the good that can result.

Sylvania,

May 29, 2009

11/20/00

Dear Mrs. Gorman,
My name is Maureen Connolly.
You spoke at Seaholm High
school in 1999, when I was a
freshman in the FLEX program.
After hearing you speak, I
was so moved that I wrote
you the enclosed letter.
While I am a little
embarassed by the dramatic
nature of my words, I still
look back on your visit
as one of the most influen[tial]
events of my life. As I
promised in my letter, I['m]
writing to inform you of
how your story has shaped
my life and inspired me
to reach out to others:
I graduated from Harvard
in June with a degree in
psychology. I am curren[tly]
applying to medical school
where I hope to study
AIDS and women's health

...rman,
I would like to thank you for ...
...ne Junior High School. My nam...
... very inspiring person. You live...
...hrough. But to imagine a little gi...
...states me. You are a very strong w...
...eighth grade class, you words s...
...ankful to have the things I ha...
...work safe and sound. I did...
... with a mother, no fath...
... thought about my...
... couldn't imag...

... are a ...

were...
Gorm...

grateful ...
hiding for ...
food, water, ...
if there wasn...
more. Your st...
their life shoul...
possible. You sa...
muscles were so w...
your story my "tush...
complaining about m...
me that since you hid...
miracle that you actually had a person nice enough to let you stay in their barn and hid...
from the Nazi's.

...o years it must have been torture for you, but almost a...
...urting when you sat on yours for two years? It seem[s]...
...of the barn. And then it hit me. Why am I...
...badly. And then it hit me. Why am I...
...almost two years and know that anyth...
...and know that anything...
...ars facing challe...
...e gun but...
...that yo...
...Well while I was listening...
...listening...

Mrs. Gorman you are my hero, I look up to you. You have been through the
unimaginable and you seem like you are unbreakable. I just wanted to say thank you so
much for coming down to Timberstone and telling us your amazing life story. Your story
made me realize that anything is capable of happening again.

Love,

Haven Hol...

...ven Holdridge Lo...

Dear Mrs. Gorman,

Thank you so much for coming to talk to our eighth grade class at
really appreciate the time you took out of your day to tell us your story and lessons you
wanted us to learn. I will always remember how you called us your wild flowers. I will
also remember when you said "touschi" because I am also Jewish, and I knew exactly
what you were talking about before you explained it to everyone.

developing countries (I actually
wrote one of my application
essays about your visit).
But before I start medical
school, I will spend a year
in the Dominican Republic
working with young girls
and sex workers who have
AIDS. I won a fellowship
from Harvard to pay for
my time abroad and I plan
to leave in January.

I hope this letter finds
you well. Even though you
have never met me, you
have had a huge impact
on my life. Thank you!

Sincerely,
Maureen
Connolly
age 23

*Some of the letters I've received
over the years; the one in the
center from Maureen Connolly
is one of my favorites.*

Park Blvd
617

We
Mrs.

r
ou,

little kids wh
I've learned
already own.
everything a
taken for gr
me, I feel
see ther
to see
tell people

be nice to others and to treat others the way you
ed that being mean and judging
ose people. You also taught m
blood" example really made
r people or treat them differ

had to, and that just tells
what we have right now
t we have is amazing.
mal. Your talk has rea
g the time to talk to

Sincerel

Sincerely yours,

ear Mrs. Gorman,

I am writing this letter to you to thank you for taking time out of your day to share your story.

I learned a lot from listening to you speak. It really introduced me to a new way of thinking. At first when I heard you were coming, I have to be honest, I thought it would be really boring and pointless. But, just listening to you words and hearing you experiences was life changing. You told us not to feel sorry for you, but I can't help feeling sorry. It made me appreciate everything I have, like running water and a loving family, so much more. I don't think, if I went through everything that you went thought, that I would be able to go on. I would have so much hate in me. I have read books about the Holocaust and seen movies but I just didn't seem real, but listening to you made everything real. Meeting somebody and hearin...

imagine what you went ...

4350 Cranberry Lane
Sylvania, OH 43560
June 8, 2009

---

ear Mrs. Gorman,

I would like to thank you for sp
t the atrocities that you saw durin
xperienced must be difficult but
re is no place in the world for p
ecause of their race, religion,
d the other things that I take

world needs more people
g hand no matter what th
hink that another Holoc
now, in the Darfur reg
nating money or givi
ake the best attemp
r time to speak to m

Dearest Mrs. Gorman,

I am writing to thank you for visiting and speaking to the Timberstone eighth grade class. I learned so much from your talk with us.

I will tell you how I felt and what I took away from all of it. I think that the messages you brought forth were just remarkable.

You told us at the beginning that we were all your little flowers, your very different flowers. That made me very happy and honored. The flower reference made me already start to envision your personality. You came off as bright, warm and strong. Then suddenly your life story came in...like a major awakening. As it transformed how I noticed how so well off" into "hiding under the floorboards of the prison building" I noticed how serious a talk you were giving us. If you saw a sore tushie in the audience or a sour expression on a face you lovingly corrected those who had been fidgety.

Also, you stayed noticeably calm throughout the whole speech. I admire you for your strength. Sometimes I thought I had it bad. Call it teenage rebellion and all that. Then suddenly, after hearing you, it was like all of a sudden (cliché as it sounds) everything I have is a blessing. I learned to be less spoiled and more grateful. Otherwise...I might forget what's important.

Of course, the greatest and most true message of all was the one regarding the realism of prejudice. It has existed for years and years and sadly still does exist in cruel, uncaring hearts. When I see someone as bright and shiny as you, someone who went through so much just because of the hate and tyranny of one man...I think...why didn't anyone try and stop him? But then I remember how many people believed in his terrible message and supported him, and I shudder. If I ever see that kind of person he was begin to rise again...I'll be the first to get up and resent it.

Though I can't say I know what you've been through, I feel for you. I hope that your message beats through the hearts of all students and the world for all eternity.

Sincerely Yours,

Sanya Ali

---

h grade
to hav
work safe and
with a mothe
thought abo
uldn't im
I w
lot o
ry
dange
your
mys

June 8, 2009

...hth grade Timberstone class

...Remembering the tragedies that

...story. Your story has showed me

...kind and that no one should be

...m also no more grateful for my

...as running water and having space

...ho helped you. I will always try to

...ty. I believe that the citizens of the

...But, I believe that one is

...mericans must help the people of

...member your speech for the rest of

...rejudiced. Thank you again for

Sincerely,

Colin H. Lee

Colin H. Lee

Mrs. Gorman,

Hello, my name is Kayla Maseman. I am writing to than...
coming to our school. I enjoyed your speech and hearing you stor...
personally enjoyed it because my grandmother also lived in Fran...
during the war. I always loved to hear her stories.

Your speech was very powerful, and meaningful. It is hard for...
to imagine that such a time occurred. How someone could be so hear...
isn't that much different, with all the murders, kidnappings, and so...
judgmental, and cruel can be, and then I realized our society today...
many terrible things that one can do. Other horrible actions are school
shootings. Its not the popular cheerleaders, or the jocks, or even the
bullies whose fingers pull the trigger it's the people who I have been cut
down and hurt so many times that they don't feel welcome or safe in
their own school.

After hearing you story I thought about how lucky we are with
new clothes, running water, our iPods, and TVs that we don't think
t what it would be like without them. I have been
aised to not judge and that if a joke is hurting somebody then it's
ny.
ank you again for coming to Timberstone to talk to us about
y. I loved being one of your flowers.

Sincerely,

Kayla Maseman

8154 B...
Toledo, C...
June 8, 2...

Dear Mrs. Gorman,

I am writing to thank for visiting Timberstone and telling us about your ...
have really made me understand that nobody no matter what size race or ethnicity ...
person is, they should never be bullied or teased because everybody is the same on th...
inside and the outside really does not matter. I also want to thank you for really letting ...
know how hard it was then. I did not realize how much Jews had to go through just to
stay alive. It would be really tough to hide under boards and be quiet at night when Nazi
are coming. It would be even harder to stand there and watch my mother die without
emotions. Also me and my friends used to complain if we don't have pop in our house, but since you have spoken to us we realize how
or if we don't have the newest games
good we have it now and we do not complain as much, and for you to live and survive
like that I really Respect you. Again, thank you for coming and I hope u keep moving on
strong with your life, and one day I hope I can be as strong as you.

Sincerely

Jino Vergiel

To...
June ...

...words sa...

I have. I was gla...

...n't get that aggravated fe...

Sometimes I would think about hi...

...and I. But I'm thankful to have a mother an...

...without them.

...let you know that you are my hero; and my mother as...

...no can be heroes, like Firemen, Police, Coast Guard

...t you survived the extraordinary, which makes y...

...was younger and didn't understand much. And

...men around that age. You went to work at

...same time. I haven't got a paid job, yet

...ver really got to be a kid or live a norm...

The Ishpeming School Experience

In the late 1990s, teachers Carole Turner and Joe Pelkola from C. L. Phelps Middle School in Ishpeming, Michigan, went to Washington, D.C. They visited the United States Holocaust Memorial Museum, and they became enthralled with what they witnessed and learned there. When they came home, the teachers contacted the Holocaust Memorial Center in suburban Detroit, eager to know more about this horrific event.

Upper left: One of many projects created by students at Phelps Middle School. Background: Students, parents, and members of the community attend the school's Holocaust program. Lower right: A program cover.

After attending a class at the center, they decided to teach about the Holocaust in their school, and they asked the center if anyone was available to speak to their classes. Most of the speakers didn't want to travel that far; Ishpeming is in Michigan's Upper Peninsula, a full eight-hour drive from the Detroit area.

Martin Lowenberg, a fellow survivor, was a salesman who traveled throughout the state, so he felt comfortable making the trip in order to tell his story. After a few years, however, the teachers felt they needed someone to help share the speaking responsibilities, and they asked Martin if he could find a child survivor to speak. The center recommended me. I figured I'd try it once; little did I know that this would become an annual trip for me!

The Holocaust program was more than just a unit of study for the students; it expanded across the entire school curriculum into an eight-week interdisciplinary experience involving music, writing, theater, and other classes, becoming an annual community-wide event. The students, mostly seventh graders, were assigned to use the Internet and other resources to research a particular person, object, or story related to the Holocaust, and then use their findings to create a display or presentation. Because of the support of their inspirational teachers, the enthusiastic students became immersed in their work. Their displays transformed the entire school into a museum for several days. Each child stood in front of his or her display, explaining the project and answering questions from visitors. Parents and others in the community were also very involved, helping to make wall hangings, replicas of concentration camps, and other visual aids. Students from other schools visited to see the displays. Some students wrote and performed plays. One play was based on my story, complete with a makeshift barn. Some students wrote poetry, and the best poems were selected to be recited to an audience. A large student orchestra performed works by Jewish composers and music played in concentration camps. Once, I saw a couple of children in wheelchairs who were part of the performance; I was pleased to see this special effort on their part. Then Martin and I shared our stories. One year, the school superintendent presented me with an honorary high school diploma; I even wore a cap and gown! On the final day of each year's event, between 600 and 700 people, including students, parents and guests, participated in a pot-luck dinner. Throughout all of these events, parents often came to tell me how their child seemed to change while working on the project. Although school budgets were tight, the district superintendent had approved funding for the project in part because of its long-term effects: some teachers and administrators had observed that, when the students got to high school, those who had studied the Holocaust curriculum were more gentle, more tolerant of others, and more aware about what was happening in the world.

Some of the children in the community served by Phelps Middle School are very poor and experience a variety of family problems. During my visits, I asked the teachers to point out children who needed a little extra

155

THE ISHPEMING SCHOOL EXPERIENCE

attention so I could gravitate towards them and talk to them, give a hug, or otherwise try to make them feel good. I told the students, "When I was in the first grade, it would have helped me if someone had been nice to me. It's so nice if each one of you would give a hug to the person who is the least liked in your school." And they always got it. The response is always great. How long the effect lasts, I don't know. Sometimes kids came back from the high school to say hello to me, and I find that incredible. They didn't have to do that. Two of them in particular have maintained contact with me over the years.

In 2005, the National Middle School Association (NMSA) recognized the team of middle-school teachers at Phelps Middle School for their work with the Holocaust curriculum. The teachers were selected as one of four "Teams That Make a Difference" honorees. The description of the award on the NMSA website states,

> The Holocaust unit has improved the citizenship of most of the students that have taken part in the unit. There have been no fights in the building in the past eight years. Using their own conflict resolution skills, the students have realized the need to be more tolerant of others. The emotions brought about by studying the prejudice, hatred, stereotyping and racism cause the students to look inside of themselves and make real life choices of how they will treat other people. In reflection upon a lesson using literature circles, students commented that they

enjoyed working with students they do not normally associate with because it gave them the opportunity to get to know these students. This response showed a more tolerant attitude toward peers, and additional proof that our students are more open and not as likely to prejudge people.

In 2008, I learned the unfortunate news that, although the school is still teaching the Holocaust, the scale of the event has been severely limited, I assume due to funding cuts and teacher layoffs. However, I remain inspired by the community and the effort made by the teachers. I hope the Ishpeming program can continue again in the future because it certainly was a success story and impacted many lives ... for the better!

Suzanne and Her Family

Although we experienced the horrible events of the war and its aftermath together, my sister Suzanne's life turned out much different than mine. When my father and I made the decision to leave France and move permanently to the United States, Suzanne felt abandoned and devastated, even though she was married with a life of her own. Many years afterwards, she spoke to me about what it was like to be left behind. She already felt separated from the family in Metz and the Jewish community because of her political beliefs.

Suzanne and Bernard Spiegelmann, with their daughter Martine and son Fernand, in 1989.

One time I recall her lamenting that her children grew up without aunts, uncles, and cousins because we were in the United States and her family had no interaction with the French relatives. She felt totally isolated. I believe this may have contributed to her feelings of inferiority and her desire to pursue material security.

My nephew Fernand was born in 1953, soon after my father and I left. He had a heart condition, and Suzanne frequently had to rush him to the hospital. She had no family to support her at the time except her husband, Bernard. Undoubtedly, she felt very alone without us there to help her. My niece Martine was born in 1960, and she was also quite frail. So once again, my sister was without her extended family to help her cope.

Bernard had a sister who was put in an insane asylum after she saw her family murdered in 1942 or 1943. The war had caused Bernard and his family to flee Metz, going to the south of France to the so-called "free area." However, most of the family members were eventually rounded up, and Bernard's sister apparently watched the others being murdered or taken away. She became ill with grief and was taken to a hospital, which likely saved her from the same fate as the rest of her family. She was later transferred to an asylum, where she remained until around 2002, when she was put into a group home. I believe no one in the family had any contact with her after the war except for Bernard, who visited her on occasion. She was "lost" to everyone. My niece and nephew didn't even know they had an aunt until the late 1990s, perhaps because their parents were ashamed of the stigma of mental illness or did not want to burden their children with this knowledge.

Suzanne herself could probably have benefited from counseling, even as early as our return to France after the war. My sister was not well educated, however, and she was too proud to admit she needed help. Nowadays, things are different; there is no stigma for people who seek therapy in order to deal with their problems. Back then, people either hid or denied their own or their loved ones' mental or emotional problems.

Although I tried to talk with my sister about our experiences on more than one occasion, she was unwilling, probably to protect herself rather than protect me. She didn't want to open a Pandora's box like I did when I started therapy. She was already unhappy, and I think she was afraid that if she did explore her feelings, it would be more than she could bear. She never got the help she needed. Perhaps this was due to her husband, who seemed almost ashamed to admit the need for psychiatric help, even though he had been a medical student before the war.

My early memories about my sister are vague, likely because of the six-year difference in our ages. Maybe if my sister had been more willing to recall and share her memories, I might have more information today, but she only agreed to talk to me about what happened to us on three occasions, when I visited her in France in the late 1990s. I know she loved me, but because my father and I left for the United States over forty years earlier, the closeness and personal friendship were never there.

I had been in therapy for many years when Suzanne went into a deep depression. I sent her a French book about depression written by a woman who noted that it took years to finally find the right doctor to treat her. She wrote about never giving up the search for the right person to work with, and I wanted Suzanne to feel more comfortable about seeking help. I also sent the book to each of Suzanne's children because I thought they had no real understanding of her pain, what she went through, and why she became what she was. Suzanne never got professional help.

Indeed, Suzanne couldn't shake the "victimness" of her life. I think I was luckier because I did seek help and had the support of my family during the many years of therapy. To this day, I have guilt feelings about her. She didn't say goodbye to me as she was dying from cancer, and I don't know why. When I went to see her a couple of times before she died, she wanted me to crawl into bed with her, but I couldn't. I felt she was asking a lot, and I was unable to give that to her at that time. Usually, she would become tense if she were touched by anyone other than her daughter, whom she adored. I have this feeling of guilt that I angered her when she saw I couldn't give her the support she needed, even though I had supported her from afar all my life. I was very supportive when her husband was dying, but her imminent death I couldn't deal with.

I recently asked my niece whether my sister's grave is kept up, and she assured me that it was. I wanted to know if my niece and nephew had reconciled themselves with their mother's death. It's important to me that my family's graves be maintained.

Suzanne is very present on my mind. I always blame myself for whatever happens.

Child Holocaust

articipants come from 20 countries

lice and vermin."

This week in Jerusalem, Blitzer, now Erna Gorman, joined dozens of other child Holocaust survivors to share stories and keep the memories alive. Participants at the con-

BY AR
THE ASS

JERU
5-year
France
older s
visit rel
never m

She v
Nazis f
During
her mo
forced
of his v
family a

chil-
ly of
par-

long
and-
eek's
World
hild

ages
nch
oy o
e pa
ure

Erna and her older sister survived by hiding in a barn in where they could not

workshops and discussio
aimed at reuniting long-lo
friends and guaranteeing th
their dramatic tales out

Esther Grebler

Although Suzanne was mostly unable and unwilling to discuss the details of our experiences with me, I was fortunate to have another source of information who was able to corroborate and fill in the gaps of some of my memories: Esther Grebler. She is the young family friend who we accidentally discovered while following the Russian soldiers near the end of the war, just a few days after my mother's death. When I reunited with Esther in 2007, she was able to enlighten me on why my family went to Monasterzyska, my mother's home town, in 1941. My father's home town had already been cleared of Jews, and Monasterzyska was still held by the Russians. So my parents probably took us there because they thought we'd be safe.

Upper left: Esther Grebler and me in Jerusalem after our reunion in 2007. Background: Newspaper coverage of the conference at which I met up with Esther. Lower left: Me, my father, Esther, and Suzanne, in France after the war. I received the dress I am wearing from the Red Cross.

My family and the Greblers met there and became friends. Esther and my sister went together to the Russian school in the town for a short while, until the Germans took over. Maybe this is where I learned to speak Russian, although Esther doesn't recall me going to school.

Esther was about the same age as my sister and the only child in her family. She and her parents had previously lived with her mother's family in Czortków, Ukraine. Her mother had an older brother with two children. Esther's father was the youngest of eleven children from a nearby town, and on weekends, the families visited each other. Esther was the youngest grandchild on both sides of her family. She was only nine in 1939 and doesn't remember a lot of details from the early years of the war. For example, she doesn't remember moving to Monasterzyska, but she thinks her family went there for the same reasons my family did: because it was a larger city and the Russians were still in control of the area, thus they thought they'd be safe. Her family lived in a small flat with just one room and a kitchen. They didn't have money, so they paid their way with gold jewelry. Esther and her parents worked in the tobacco fields, growing, picking, and preparing the tobacco to send it to the government. It was dirty work, and the smell was horrible. She doesn't remember my mother clearly, but she does have an image of her as a tall and beautiful woman.

When the Germans took over Monasterzyska, the town was made into a ghetto. In the beginning, ghetto life was tolerable, but soon harsh laws restricting Jews were

implemented and the *Judenrat* was formed. Esther be-
lieves that her father might have been a part of the *Judenrat* committee, since her parents were intellectual
people. Conditions for the Jews rapidly declined. A number of Hungarian Jews were brought into the ghetto, but
she doesn't know where they originally lived. When the
Aktionen started, Esther and her family hid wherever they
could, in underground bunkers or sometimes in an attic.
Occasionally, our families were hiding together. She
remembers hiding with my sister; although she doesn't
remember me, I must have been there too. Esther remembers one bunker that was dug under the big stove in
the middle of a room; it was big enough to hold everyone
in the house. Esther was so small that during one *Aktion*,
her mother was able to save her by pushing her into the
chimney. During another raid, everyone in the house was
discovered and taken away except for Esther and her
mother, who had been in a different hiding spot. Eventually, the Germans cleared Monasterzyska and sent everyone to Buczacz, including our two families.

In Buczacz, Esther's family created yet another hiding place in the bedroom of the house where they lived.
When a house had a hiding place, it was important to
open the doors during an *Aktion* so the Germans would
be fooled into thinking everyone had fled. However,
during one of the *Aktionen* in the spring of 1943, everything happened so fast that there wasn't enough time to
open the doors, even though people were hidden in the
bunker. The Germans searched the house, and although
they could not initially find the bunker, they continued

looking because they knew people were hiding some-where inside. It took all day and into the evening, but after the Germans dug from outside the house, they discovered the people and pulled them out, one by one. Esther's mother gave her a gold watch and told her to run and hide somewhere else. Esther managed to crawl under a bed and was not discovered. Her mother and all the others were taken to the forest to be shot and buried in a mass grave. Esther's father had been out of the house during this *Aktion,* but she did not know where he was, so she was left all alone.

Esther knew some people in the town and went to them begging for help. She looked even younger that she was, and this seemed to elicit kindness from others. One Ukrainian woman who lived alone took Esther in for protection and to help find her father. The woman finally located Esther's father in a building that had been converted into a prison. Esther went to the prison and somehow got close enough so that she was able to talk with her father through a window. He gave her the name of another individual who would help her and give her a place where she could stay. He said that after the war, he would find her. A few days later, another Ukrainian woman who Esther knew took her to a place where she saw her father walking with a group of people. Esther thought the men were being taken to a work assignment and wanted to run to him, but the woman held her back because she knew the people were going to be murdered. Everyone knew. The woman hiding Esther later found out that the whole group of men had been killed near the same place where Esther's mother had died.

The Ukrainian woman took Esther to stay with the woman's mother, who was a farmer near Buczacz. Esther helped work the farm, but people eventually started asking questions about her identity, and even though the woman said Esther was her niece, people's suspicions made it unsafe for her to stay. When Esther heard Buczacz was going to be *judenfrei,* or cleared of Jews, she went to Czortków and found an aunt who took her in, but soon that area was also unsafe. Eventually, Esther made her way to Tarnopol, where she stayed in a work camp. There she helped make clothing for the Germans and was given a minimal amount of food. In 1944, Esther and another friend who spoke the local dialect decided to run away. They didn't "look Jewish," so they thought someone might be willing to help them. They met a group in the forest who told them everyone in the work camp had been killed. Esther and her friend continued walking for many days until they eventually came to another work camp where the people tended cows in the fields and also prepared food for the Germans. Somehow the girls arranged to stay and work in the camp.

In the winter of 1944, the Russians came back into the area. Esther remembers the confusion on the road, although she's not exactly sure where she was. There were many bombed out buildings, and she hid in a corner of one of them; this is where my father found her scavenging. She told him about her parents' fate, and he told her about my mother's death. He said to her, "You're coming with us, you're not staying alone." Esther joined our family and stayed with us as we followed the Russians for several months.

Esther's memories about this period are more vivid than mine, since she was older. As a result of the vermin, she had almost all the same diseases I had. She remembers that when we had scabs all over our bodies, the Russians tried to help us by having us pee into a pot so that we could wash ourselves with the urine, as this would supposedly help the scabs heal. Earlier when she lived in Monasterzyska, Esther had typhoid; she said my father also had typhoid during this period. The Russians put Esther and Suzanne into the local school as we moved from village to village, which is amazing to me. Esther and Suzanne were the best of friends.

After the Russians took us by train to Katowice, other organizations helped with our care. We were deloused and given food. The four of us were assigned to a little room where we lived together. Papa regularly visited one of the organizations that would give him a little food or a little money so he could buy us food. We slept and cooked in that one room. Esther remembers us sleeping on the floor, with straw for our beds.

In Katowice, Papa contacted a committee providing assistance to the Jewish community to see what to do about Esther. He knew that she had an aunt in Palestine (Israel), so he had her traced and contacted; the aunt was thrilled that someone in her family had survived! The relative sent paperwork for Esther to go to Palestine, a process that took several months. In the meantime, we made arrangements to go back to France. Papa found an orphanage that agreed to take Esther and provide schooling for her until we left for France. The orphanage had been established especially for children who had lost their families during the war. Esther still has pictures from the orphanage as well as documents stating that she was extremely bright and needed advanced schooling. My cousin Morty Balsam, who now lives in Florida, was in school with her, and Esther remembers him very well. After Esther and my family returned to France, Esther got her papers, and she left for Palestine.

Once in Palestine, she performed so well academically that she was able to skip many grades. Later she was drafted into the army and fought in the War of Independence in 1948, after which Israel became a nation. She eventually became a physician's assistant and really enjoyed the work. She then went to nursing school and became a surgical nurse. She was good in math and science, so she took engineering courses as well. In those days, the hospitals in Jerusalem didn't have adequate operating rooms, so she was sent to tour Europe to learn how to organize and properly equip operating rooms. Upon her return, she helped establish twenty operating rooms at various hospitals. When the Six Day War broke out in 1967, she and a crew of doctors and nurses went to the front lines to take care of the wounded. During the First Lebanon War in 1982, she went to the front again.

During this time, she married a Jewish German physician who had two young children. They had another child together. In the early 1990s, however, she and her husband split.

She never spoke about her past to others. After she first went to Israel, she corresponded with my sister, although at the time, I was not aware of this. As the two of them got busy with their lives, however, their letters to each other stopped.

In 2007, I attempted to locate Esther. I didn't know whether she was even still alive. I contacted a hidden-children organization in Israel that was able to track her down and give me her phone number. I immediately called her, and we were both overjoyed to rediscover each other. We decided to meet in person at my hotel during my visit to Jerusalem to attend the Hidden Children Conference. Of course, I didn't know what she looked like after all of these years, but I had with me an old photo of her with my family. I sat in the hotel lobby with that picture, checking out every woman who came in. My friends from Detroit wouldn't leave me by myself until Esther arrived. When she finally came in the door, she saw the photo and ran toward me. It was so moving because she said she also has the same photo. Over sixty years had passed since our brief time together during and after the war, yet here we were, meeting again. Amazing! She related to me her experiences, many of which we went through together. She confirmed many of my memories, such as those of hunger and the constant fear in the ghettos.

Esther speaks perfect English because Palestine was still under the control of the British when she emigrated, so her schooling was in English. She gave up speaking all other languages. I asked her if she ever went back to Poland, and she replied, "How could I ever go back there?" That's how I feel, too. I probably wouldn't recognize anything anyway. I asked her if she knew where we might have been hidden or where we buried my mother, but she couldn't tell me anything about that. I asked her how long she thinks we were hidden in the barn, in hopes that my father had told her. She said she thinks it was a year and a half or more, but she wasn't entirely sure. In 2008, Esther came to visit her daughter in Vancouver, British Columbia. I had planned to go visit her, but instead I had hip replacement surgery! I would rather have been in Vancouver!

My conversations with Esther validated one important thing for me: I didn't just dream my childhood memories. I didn't dream the nightmare.

*My family in December 2009. From left: Oldest son Mark, granddaughter Lily,
me and Herb, granddaugher Sydney, son Robert, granddaughter Julia, and
daughter-in-law Ruth. (Photo by Jim Goddell.)*

Reflections

A by-product of putting my story down on paper has been the many memories and random thoughts that pop into my mind at the most curious times. I feel it's important to record them, not because they are part of a chronological story, but because they represent my reflections and feelings about my life and what happened to me.

I feel as though I had a good and happy life until it was destroyed for me, in a sense, when I awoke to my repressed memories of the horrific events of my childhood. After that, my life could never be the same. Maybe with this book complete, I will be able to devote my time to thinking about something else besides the Holocaust. But my memories seem to plague me from morning till night. I wish I could return to the years of looking at the flowers; I was much better off when I didn't remember any of this. I know that other Holocaust survivors are also haunted by their memories the same way I am.

All I have left, then, is to try to understand and make sense of the various aspects of my life—my experiences, my relationships, and my decisions. A big part of that involves my father. My post-war life was terrible. For a time, I was filled with anger towards him. He did so much for Esther, finding relatives, arranging for schooling, and helping send her to Israel. He was a hero for her. I didn't have the same kind of positive feelings for him, however. I realize that he and my mother endured a constant struggle to save us, but I have never *felt* the emotional impact of that the way I suppose I should have. When Esther talked about my father, she spoke with fondness. She probably would have made her way to Israel regardless of his help, but certainly his involvement at such a crucial time in her life influenced her feelings for him. I did not feel that same tenderness, that feeling of love. Life was difficult for me in the post-war years, and perhaps my feelings are overwhelmingly affected by that experience. I don't know. I do recall one time in Metz, after the war,

176

when I was so hungry that I began to cry. He cried, too.
How strange it was for me to see him crying when neither
of us cried at my mother's death. I know he would have
killed someone for me. I know that for sure. He loved me.
Yet I was angry with him. I was obedient, and I felt a
sense of responsibility for him, but there was no tenderness. The French word *devoir* pops into my mind. It means
duty, but it also conveys the idea of fate. This complex re-
lationship with my father was my fate. Perhaps it's wrong
that I don't see him in the same light as Esther does. My
parents *were* heroes, absolute heroes, and I never would
have survived without them. As the years have gone by, I
have come to terms with my many emotions and no
longer feel anger towards my father. I understand him
(and myself) much better, and I miss him now.

Another notable theme of my reflections is survival.
It is mind-boggling to me now how many times I should
have died but didn't. How can it be that I was so fortunate, so lucky to survive, even though the odds were
against me? The people who survived the concentration
camps were tended to be late-comers to those places.
Most of the people who went there in 1942 or 1943 died
before the war ended. For example, my friends Ruth Web-
ber and Paula Lebovics, both of whom survived the
Auschwitz children's block, likely made it because on the
day they arrived, there was no selection process. When I
think about our individual experiences, I feel like I'm the
lucky one because Ruth and Paula had to be in that hell
called Auschwitz. In the beginning of my therapy, I had
such guilt feelings because I did survive. I felt I belonged

in the oven. The guilt trip was masochistic; my pain was bad, but yet I felt it should have been worse. Every survivor's experience is unique. Once at a meeting of hidden children, I met a camp survivor who felt that we had suffered more than she had because we were isolated, whereas she was with other children. Survivors typically feel that other survivors' experiences are worse than their own.

For a recent article written about me, I was asked what my feelings are now about my survival. I once again asked myself, why did I survive? It's because a Christian helped us and risked his own life. I have never blamed Christians for the Holocaust; I am here now because of a Christian. People seem to forget about this. Most of the survivors were helped by a Christian at some point. It's a very important but often neglected point that most of us hidden children survived because a Christian decided to make a difference. I think the majority of people have goodness in them, regardless of their religious beliefs.

I have also had to come to terms with what I call my "lost years." In the time immediately following the war, I was often bewildered. Yes, I was very fortunate that I had survived, but now what? The world and what it had to offer was totally unknown to me as an eleven-year-old girl. Not one person tried to help me discover what potential I might have had. Instead, I had to work, cook, and clean our cramped living space. The days blended one into the other. I am not bitter or looking to place blame. I only feel sorrow for those lost years. I did not know how important education was or would be for me. I shrunk from learning because I was afraid that my mind was not capable of doing so. I envy the ones that had the nurturing and foresight to pursue their education.

Fortunately, however, I took advantage of an opportunity for a new start when I came to the United States. Finally, I had escaped. In fact, that's when I feel as though I was truly born and began to flourish; my arrival in the States marked the actual beginning of my life. Both my father and I were able to start over. He went to work at a Ford factory and was able to put his life together without the struggle of daily survival. I fell in love, got married, and had a family and a life.

I am fortunate to have assembled a collection of artifacts, documents, and photos from my early life, but my most precious treasure I have is my mother's purse. In fact, it is the only thing I have that belonged to her. It is amazing that the purse survived at all. Apparently, when my parents originally left France on their trip to Poland, my mother left her purse behind, and it came into the care of my aunt. How and why she managed to preserve the purse is a mystery, but it was given to me many years later. One of the few photos I have of my mother shows her with this purse. It is very important to me.

In reconciling my memories and experiences, I have been compelled to talk about the horrors of World War II and the dangers of allowing a dictatorship of such magnitude and evil to exist. I was lucky enough to survive such evil. It's as if my survival was a gift given to me, and I am obligated to repay others for this gift. Should the repayment be to the point where I feel everything so intensely every day of my life? I do have balance in my life but not sufficiently enough that I can be totally happy. I'm often asked if sharing my experience is cathartic for me. Do I feel better after I talk about it? Hell, no. That's why I don't think what I'm experiencing is normal. I asked my psychiatrist, "Why am I this way?" He said that for some people, once the memories are awakened, they stay with them for the rest of their lives. Still, I cannot say that I am entirely sure of all the reasons why I feel the need to talk about my experiences. I wonder if there is a need in me to inflict some sort of self-punishment. Maybe I feel I need to be punished because I had so many things happen to me that were happy. Ultimately, I am a happy person, thanks to the love of my husband, children, and grandchildren, and my many friends. Perhaps I just want to boast about being different. Do I just need to hear myself say these things over and over? Even my psychiatrist doesn't know. He doesn't think such factors are driving my desire to tell my story, but I still question my motives.

Regardless, with the completion of this book, I hope to stop thinking about the Holocaust. I am ready to not think about making a speech but instead to think about going to the theatre or to a concert, or to look at the flowers or weed my flower beds—I am ready to move on.

I *need* to release the past and look to the flowers. I need to limit my contacts related to the Holocaust. I now regularly refuse requests to speak that in years past I would have granted. However, I know that many are drawn to ask me to tell my story because they think that, through me, the audience can experience the Holocaust in a way not portrayed in museums and books — to hear such a story from a real human being has great impact. In addition, I don't just relay my basic story; I emphasize what prejudice and hatred can do to an individual, helping them apply lessons from the Holocaust in a broader way. I can judge this by the many letters I receive from those who have heard me speak. The majority say I made them realize that they should be a little more watchful about prejudice against others. My audiences do get my point, and that's what I'm pleased about. I inspire them to see that life can be different, if we want to make it different. Society doesn't owe us anything. We must do for ourselves.

It is natural for young people to live in their cocoons and not concern themselves with the rest of the world. I want young people to see that what is truly important to me is how I have tried to minimize hatred and prejudice in my life. I don't want them to forget that there is pain everywhere in the world. They cannot just sweep this away because it doesn't concern them personally. Young people today see a lot of violence in movies and computer games, so they may not be able to perceive that others are indeed really hurt; I am concerned that they are not able to feel or understand pain in others. They have become indifferent to real violence and real suffering. The truth of the matter is that we can't live only for our own pleasure; we must extend a hand to our neighbor. Most kids today probably don't know the horror that is going on in Africa, for example. How could we allow the Tutsis and the Hutus to murder each other? How could the world allow this to happen? Is it because we have no financial interest in those countries? Is everything governed by the wealth a country has to offer? Don't we as humans have a duty to care for each other? What makes us different from animals? Animals kill when they are threatened or hungry, but humans kill for ambition, to feel superior, for monetary gain, or for pleasure. Religion has become a crutch, an excuse for why we do things, but it's ultimately about power. I don't want people to think that I am totally without prejudice. I'm not even sure that's possible. That's not what I want to portray. Unless we do for one another, however, we might lose hope and our humanity.

I am very mindful of the impact my story may have on succeeding generations. If I had been actively thinking about the Holocaust all my life and speaking about it to my children, they might have grown up to see the world in an embittered light. I've heard presentations by and about children of survivors who were affected by the fact that their parents relived the war every day. The first time I heard second-generation children speak was at a conference in Seattle. Some of the anger that came out was horrifying to me. I saw a young woman who was sitting by herself, so I joined her. We started talking, and her anger immediately began pouring out. Suddenly, she stood up and said to the audience, "I'm representing my parents who aren't here. You don't seem to address the issue of gay people and how Holocaust survivors viewed a gay child."

She repeated this to me again, and I asked her to take a walk with me. I told her it took a lot of courage to stand up and say that in front of a group. She gave me a new viewpoint on the suffering of the second generation of Holocaust survivors. It didn't make a difference to me that she was gay; to me she was just a girl who was crying and needed help.

It seems to me that the grandchildren of survivors are more engaged in doing research about the Holocaust than their parents, who had to live every day with the pain and baggage of their own parents' experiences.

Finally, I never want the world to forget the horror of war. In Europe today, there are lovely green and wooded areas that were formerly sites of death and destruction; their beauty masks the graves that lie below. We find a way to forget what we don't want to remember. In the United States, we seem to particularly avoid thinking about such unpleasant things. For example, soldiers who served in Vietnam weren't allowed to share their memories because so many of us didn't really want to know what happened in a place so far away. I know a Green Beret who refused to talk about the things he saw and did in Vietnam. He was traumatized, and even his mother didn't know what had happened to her son. During a presentation at Marygrove College in Detroit, I commented that I didn't know how a soldier could inflict so much pain on another human being. One of the students became very quiet. He came to me afterward and said that as a Vietnam veteran, he knew firsthand that, in the heat of the battle and with fear and with training, soldiers are capable of murder and destruction and other things they would never do in normal life. He was very sad, and I was sad for him, and I think we both cried. When he came back from the war, I imagine that he was denied the freedom to talk about this. People didn't even want to know about these soldiers. Their situation was very much like ours after the Holocaust. Now it is common to interview soldiers in Iraq for the sake of drama and the news. These soldiers who come back who have been traumatized or wounded need care for the rest of their lives, but we tend to forget that they are there and in need.

Telling my story is a petrifying experience, and when I talk to strangers, I relive every moment. I am torn apart completely and absolutely as I do that. As I've already said, I'm often asked if telling my story is cathartic, and it's not. At least for me it's not. My true wish is to be done with this work, so I can be in peace. It sounds dramatic, but that's the way I feel. The intense examination that I've gone through recalling and reliving the horrors I've experienced has led me to believe that I must achieve something positive and once and for all bring finality to this nightmare. I'm looking forward to this happening, if it ever will. At least I've tried my best to make it happen.

I hope my story in some way illustrates that hatred and bigotry, when allowed to be taken to their extreme, can be both devastating and deadly. My request of those who know my story is this: Do not be a silent and passive bystander to the wrongs that you witness. Don't ignore the situation as if it doesn't exist. Be aware of the potential harm and danger that you see, and stand up to it. It takes a lot of courage, but we all, each one of us, can make a difference.

CITATION

from

Northern Michigan University

The Board of Trustees
has voted to confer the honorary degree of

Doctor of Education

upon

Erna Blitzer Gorman

A child survivor of the Holocaust, Erna Blitzer Gorman was born in Metz, France in 1934. Her father was a Jewish immigrant who came to France from Poland and her mother was from an Orthodox Jewish home in the Ukraine. In 1939, while Erna's family was visiting Poland, Germany invaded and the family was not allowed to return to France. With the disappearance of their Polish relatives at the hands of the Nazis, Erna's father moved their family to the Ukraine to live with her mother's parents. When the Nazis invaded the Ukraine, killing and deporting Jews to concentration camps, Erna's family moved to a ghetto and later fled to the woods where they met a Christian farmer who agreed to hide them. To protect his own family, the farmer did not tell his children that he was helping this Jewish family. Erna's family of four lived in a small hayloft for almost two years where they could not stand or speak aloud. The farmer's family was very poor, yet he managed to bring them food and water every night.

I n February of 1944, the Russian Red Army arrived in the Ukraine and Erna's family, unable to walk, were carried one-by-one by the farmer out of the barn so they could obtain help from the soldiers. Erna's mother was then injured, eventually dying from her wounds in a local infirmary. When the war ended, Erna, her father and her sister returned to France. Having received no formal education and unable to read or write, Erna was enrolled in school. When other children learned that she was Jewish, she became a constant target of persecution and discrimination. In 1953, Erna and her father immigrated to Detroit to live with her father's sister. Erna found work in a factory and met Herb Gorman. They married and raised two sons together; Mark, a physician who specializes in neurology at the University of Vermont and Robert, a corporate attorney in Chicago. Mr. and Mrs. Gorman have three granddaughters.

F or almost 40 years after World War II ended, Erna Blitzer Gorman did not speak of her traumatic experiences during the Holocaust to anyone. Her family knew that they should not ask questions. Erna's traumatic memories were re-activated in the 1980's after seeing neo-Nazi skin heads on television shouting they would finish what Hitler had started. She decided to tell her husband and sons what she had experienced during World War II and to speak publicly about the Holocaust.

A courageous and resilient woman who has triumphed over her own experiences, Erna Gorman has made it her mission to teach others, especially children, about the dire results of a society that promotes intolerance and discrimination. During the past 20 years, Erna has spoken to thousands of people about the importance of tolerance in society. She has spoken to students of all ages, including presentations at Bowling Green State University, the University of Michigan, Northern Michigan University and numerous elementary and high schools throughout Michigan and beyond. In fact, she has become a regular visitor to C.L. Phelps Middle School in Ishpeming, where she received an honorary diploma. When she was the Holocaust Memorial speaker in Marquette in April, 2009, she told the audience that the diploma from Phelps Middle School was the first and only educational degree she has obtained since her school years were taken away from her by World War II.

T housands of American citizens, especially students in Michigan, have been educated, enriched and enhanced by the decision of Mrs. Gorman to speak out for racial and ethnic tolerance. Through her work, she carries the message that the actions of one person, like those of the Christian farmer who saved the lives of her Jewish family, can affect many. Northern Michigan University is pleased to bestow upon Erna Blitzer Gorman the honorary degree of Doctor of Education.

Conferred this 12th day of December, 2009, at Marquette, Michigan.

Leslie E. Wong
President of Northern Michigan University

Douglas Roberts, Ph.D.
Chair, Northern Michigan University Board of Trustees

EPILOGUE

In the fall of 2009, while the draft of my manuscript for this book was being edited and other content was being pulled together, I received an e-mail from Dr. Susan J. Koch, the provost at Northern Michigan University (NMU) in Marquette, Michigan, asking me to please give her a call. When I did, I was immediately put through to her, and she said, "I have wonderful news for you. The university is offering you an honorary doctoral degree, and we are hoping you will accept." Of course, I was flabbergasted and didn't know what to say. In fact, I think I just thanked her, said good-bye, and hung up! Even though I knew I really had talked with the provost and that the offer had gone through all the proper channels at the school, I thought it was all a joke at first. I didn't know what the offer was all about.

Soon afterward, I received a letter from the provost explaining the details. If I accepted the degree, I would be honored at several events and would give the commencement speech at the university's midyear graduation ceremonies that December. The letter stated that a number of people had written recommendations on my behalf, including students and Dr. Helen Kahn, a professor at NMU. My nomination had been immediately accepted by the university's Board of Trustees and its president, Dr. Leslie Wong. The letter concluded by noting that everyone at NMU was very excited and hoped I would give them a positive answer soon.

Even after reading the letter, I still thought the offer was a joke and couldn't believe it was meant for me. Really, I didn't understand why the university was offering this to me; I kept asking myself and Herb, "Why would they do this? I haven't gone to school, I haven't done anything special. There are other people who speak." The mind couldn't accept the reality. For several days, Herb and I went back and forth—why should I say yes when there are so many other people worthy of this honor? Another letter soon arrived, urging me to accept. Everyone around me who knew of the request encouraged me to say yes, so finally, I did.

Truthfully, the idea didn't start to feel real until a few weeks before the commencement ceremony, when I finally realized that, yes, this was actually going to happen, and I needed to get serious about it. Still, it didn't feel like it was going to be me up there accepting such an honor. My emotions were mixed. I was proud that people thought I was worthy, but I was also afraid. In addition to receiving my degree in front of 2500 attendees, I also had to give a meaningful commencement speech. The thought of that was very scary! I wasn't sure I was up to it; I thought I would fail in my speech. I wasn't afraid of speaking in front of a large group; what was frightening was the thought that what I had to say wouldn't measure up to such a prestigious honor. But somehow it did—it just came out from the inside. To be truthful, I don't actually know exactly what I said that day. I have the text of the speech I prepared for the ceremony, but I spoke from my heart and occasionally strayed from my notes. At the end of my speech, I asked everybody to get up and hug the person standing next to them.

The entire weekend was wonderful. The events included a reception at Dr. Wong's lovely home, a breakfast with the honor students and their families, the commencement ceremony itself, a reception for the graduates and their families, and a dinner given in my honor by the synagogue in Ishpeming. The whole experience was so unreal. I felt just like I was floating. Whenever I have something amazing happening to me—happy or painful—I separate myself into two people. Like I'm floating. Like I'm two people.

My whole family—Herb, our sons, daughter-in-law and three granddaughters—was with me for the commencement and the accompanying festivities. What did it mean to have my family there? I was thrilled that they were proud of me. I could see this in the eyes of my grown-up children, and I could feel this by the hugs and kisses my granddaughters gave me. They wanted me not to be nervous. When I finished my speech, one of my granddaughters gave me a thumbs-up. I think they were all utterly amazed; they hadn't heard me tell my story in quite this way. My presentation gave me something to leave to my grandchildren. I'm glad that I did not embarrass them or myself, and I am proud that they were able to witness that there used to be quite a person in there. I'm not just the grandmother they know now. Many friends also traveled to attend the commencement ceremony, and it meant so much that they would think enough of me to be there. It was a very emotional but wonderful experience for all of us. After the ceremony, my granddaughters kept calling me "Dr. Nana." They still do. Some of my friends now call me "Dr. Erna," which makes me laugh.

Many emotions go through me when I think about this honor. After all, very few people get this type of recognition; it's usually an academic person or someone from a big business. I am an uneducated person, and I don't feel deserving just because I speak about my past. That sounds a little crazy, but it is true. The point is, I never expected to receive any accolades for my work, and honors of any kind make me feel uncomfortable. Herb is always thrilled for me when I receive recognition, but I am embarrassed when he tells others about the degree and the honor.

Having this honorary doctorate doesn't make me feel any different; I know it happened, and I am thrilled about it, but deep inside I don't feel as though I truly deserve it. It's not as though I feel someone finally recognized me. I am still Erna, and when I tell my story in the future, I won't mention getting the degree. It's not about how many degrees a person has, it's about what a person does with his or her life.

EPILOGUE

*Dr. Leslie Wong, left, and Dr. Susan Koch, right, present me
with my honorary degree and a citation, which is replicated
on page 186. (Photo by Camilla Mingay.)*